Cooking for Kids

Rosamond Richardson is the author of three books and presenter of the BBC TV series "Discovering Patchwork" and "Discovering Hedgerows". Born in Oxford, she now lives in Castle Hedingham, Essex, with her husband and three children.

Rosamond Richardson

Cooking for Kids

Illustrated by John Verney

JILL NORMAN

First published 1981 by Jill Norman Ltd, 90 Great Russell Street,
London WC1B 3PY

Typeset by Inforum Ltd, Portsmouth
Printed and bound in Great Britain by Mackays of Chatham Ltd
Designed by Fred Price

British Library Cataloguing in Publication Data

Richardson, Rosamond
  Cooking for Kids.
  1. Cookery
  I. Title
  641.5   TX717

ISBN 0-906908-40-X

First printing 1981

*Dedicated to the Memory of
My Mother and Father*

Acknowledgements

I am indebted to a loyal team of friends and their children who have been the guinea-pigs for most of the recipes in this book; for their support and enthusiasm as they tasted dish after dish that issued from my kitchen: especially Elizabeth Joscelyne, Liz Turner, Jeannie Ratcliff and my ever-hungry Emily. My heartfelt thanks to John Verney for his delightful drawings. They have been an inspiration to work with and have made the book such fun to look at. My gratitude to Jill Norman and Felicia Pheasant for their constructive comments and patient editorial work.

Contents

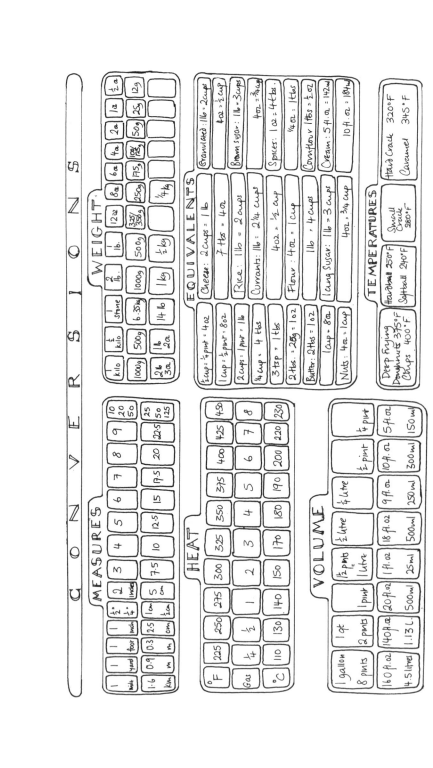

CONVERSIONS

MEASURES

				inches → cm
1 mile = 1·6 km	1 yard = 0·9 m	1 foot = 0·3 m	1 inch = 2·5 cm	

inch	½ / ¼	2	3	4	5	6	7	8	9	10 / 20 / 50
cm	1 / ½	5	7·5	10	12·5	15	17·5	20	22·5	25 / 50 / 125

WEIGHT

	½ oz	1 oz	2 oz	4 oz	6 oz	8 oz	12 oz	1 lb.	2 lb.
	12g	25g	50g	100/125g	175/200g	250g	325/350g	500g	1000g

kilo	½ kilo	500g	stone
2 lb 3 oz	1 lb 2 oz	1 lb 2 oz	6·35 kg

1 kg	½ kg	¼ kg

HEAT

°F	225	250	275	300	325	350	375	400	425	450
Gas	¼	½	1	2	3	4	5	6	7	8
°C	110	130	140	150	170	180	190	200	220	230

VOLUME

1 gallon / 8 pints	1 qt / 2 pints	1 pint	1 fl.oz
160 fl.oz / 4·5 litres	140 fl.oz / 1·13 L	20 fl.oz / 500 ml	25 ml

1½ pints / 1 litre	½ litre	¼ litre	½ pint	¼ pint
18 fl.oz / 500 ml	18 fl.oz / 500 ml	9 fl.oz / 250 ml	10 fl.oz / 300 ml	5 fl.oz / 150 ml

EQUIVALENTS

- 1 cup = ¼ pint = 4 oz
- 1 cup = ½ pint = 8 oz
- 2 cups = 1 pint = 1 lb
- ¼ cup = 4 tbs
- 3 tsp = 1 tbs
- 2 tbs = 25g = 1 oz
- Butter: 2 tbs = 1 oz
- 1 cup = 8 oz
- Nuts: 4 oz = 1 cup

- Cheese: 2 cups = 1 lb
- 7 tbs = 4 oz
- Rice: 1 lb = 2 cups
- Currants: 1 lb = 2¼ cups
- 4 oz = ½ cup
- Flour: 4 oz = 1 cup
- 1 lb = 4 cups
- Icing sugar: 1 lb = 3 cups
- 4 oz = ¾ cup

- Granulated: 1 lb = 2 cups
- 4 oz = ½ cup
- Brown sugar: 1 lb = 3 cups
- 4 oz = 3 tbs
- Spices: 1 oz = 4 tbs
- ½ oz = 1 tbs
- Cornflour: 1 tbs = ½ oz
- Cream: 5 fl.oz = 142 ml
- 10 fl.oz = 184 ml

TEMPERATURES

- Deep Frying: Doughnuts 375°F, Chips 400°F
- Hard ball 250°F
- Soft ball 240°F
- Small Crack 280°F
- Hard Crack 320°F
- Caramel 345°F

Introduction

his book is aimed at dedicated parents who spend so much of their time and energy feeding their families as they put in a thrice-daily appearance at the stove for anything up to two decades. It sounds formidable: preparing food can be an act of love, yes, but preparing food lovingly three times a day every day of the year is asking a great deal of love, let alone the stamina of the willing-but-wilting cook. Indeed it can turn out to be aversion therapy for the most enthusiastic would-be cook, and for the most devoted parent. In the possibly naïve hope of lightening this burden I decided to put pen to paper.

The philosophy behind the style of cooking in this book is that the results, tasty and wholesome as I hope they are, are achieved by labour-saving means which are still a far cry from the frozen fish-finger and the meal-in-a-bag. I have used recipes that can be made in a matter of minutes, maintaining the enthusiasm of the cook as well as the cooked-for. Many of the dishes use leftovers, too, which provide short-cuts when carefully calculated. The ingredients are widely available and store well, thus economising over time spent on the inevitable chore of shopping.

Much of the inspiration comes from my own childhood: my mother was American and her approach to cooking, and the results, were quite a contrast to that of our English friends around us. Later on in my childhood we had a series of cooks from all over the world who produced wonderful food for us. It seemed natural to pass on the essence of these varied ideas to busy parents so that they could reap the benefits from them. I have adapted them so that they are quickly prepared, and as a bonus most of them freeze very well.

The fact that children appreciate good food as much as adults is a discovery I have made while testing out my recipes not only on my small daughter but also on a wide circle of friends, young and old. So why always make the distinction between cooking for children and then again for the returning breadwinner? Many of the recipes here have been as successful with the ageing and jaded as with their children.

Children will also enjoy helping with many of the recipes in this book since a good deal of the cooking is so simple. Almost all children love to join in, and indeed helping in the kitchen is an integral part of childhood, the principal lure being the licking of fingers, and scraping the bowl when the ceremony is completed. What psychiatrist would dispute that these are experiences not to be denied the potentially balanced adult?

One aspect of life in the kitchen is the need to maintain the pleasure of cooking and eating: often if the cook is cheerful the child will enjoy the result that much more. Meal-times should be fun times, so in order to excite and involve the children I have given many of the recipes names associated with the stories and characters that make up their world. If you call it Humpty Dumplings even the fussiest of children won't stop to ask what it is.

The problem of having to cook every day is dreaming up ideas of what to have: so often one's mind draws a complete blank, and resorts to sausages yet again. In dividing up the book into small sections I have tried to make it easy to find new ideas quickly. John Verney's lively and witty illustrations make it a pleasure for parent and child alike: the aim is to make daily cooking inspired and light-hearted, and to make eating satisfying fun for all the family.

Rosamond Richardson

Handy Hints

Equipment

ne of the first necessary investments is a set of **wall scales** with both metric and imperial measures indicated: when you want to use them you pull down the tray and the weighing table is in front of your eyes. The tray is removable and washable. When not in use it is out of the way and unobtrusive on the wall. I could not have remained sane without mine while I was testing all the recipes for this book.

The second investment I recommend is an efficient **liquidiser**. Mine is big and strong and makes inimitable soups, the best breadcrumbs, and grinds nuts to perfection without a grumble. It would do anything I asked of it.

You probably possess either a **mixer** or an **electric hand-beater**. The latter is particularly useful and helps to take the agony out of baking. It cuts down on time and effort and also helps to make cakes feather-light. I could not make the cakes I do (if modesty will permit) without mine unless I were a well-trained wrestler.

A **cup measure with volume and weight equivalents** is another useful piece of equipment. They are conical-shaped and easily available. The other thing I find useful is a **thermometer** – essential for safe deep-frying. It also takes the risk out of jam-making.

Other artillery: a set of good **knives**: expensive but definitely worth it from the point of view of efficiency as well as pleasure. A **rubber scraper** to clean out bowls and saucepans. A **bulb-baster** and a **tin-opener on the wall**. And last but not least, my favourite: a **tomato knife**. It is delicate, slim and serrated and cuts all sorts of things as if they were cheese.

Collecting recipes

I have found that an excellent way of collecting recipes and keeping them in usable order is to fill up a **box-file** with cards under different categories, e.g. soups, pies, fish, salads etc. In fact, I developed this book from the collection I have made in this way from my mother's recipes, friends' ideas, cuttings from magazines, my own personal experiments and so on. The card system is easy to use and can be neatly stored in a corner of the kitchen.

Food Tips

Bacon. You can buy bacon 'pieces' at most supermarkets which are marvellous value and are all you need for many of the recipes in this book. Crisp up bacon in its own fat until it is brittle, and use the dripping for frying vegetables.

When you are wrapping bacon around something, first stretch it with the back of a knife on a wooden board until it is half the thickness and twice the length. It makes a more delicate morsel.

Breadcrumbs. I use breadcrumbs a lot in cooking, both as a topping and as an ingredient. I keep my leftovers and crusts in a plastic bag in the refrigerator, and when I have enough I liquidise them and dry them in a slow oven. The best way to keep them from going mouldy is to store them in an open bowl in a cool place like the larder, or in a plastic bag in the fridge. You can also freeze them.

As alternatives to breadcrumbs as a topping you can use crumbled cheese biscuits, wheatgerm or crushed potato crisps.

Butter. I have quoted the use of butter throughout the book (meaning unsalted), but of course it is possible to substitute margarine. Indeed, for the Topping Teas recipes soft margarine is almost an improvement. It is easier to handle than butter, makes for very light baking, and is also noticeably cheaper than butter.

You can keep your Gruyère! give me Cheddar!

Cheese. I find that Cheddar makes very good cooking cheese and is popular with the family. However, you can substitute Jarlsberg or Gruyère, Cheshire or Double Gloucester, or Mozzarella (which needs to be sliced, not grated). Parmesan is in my opinion the best of the hard cheeses and I have mentioned it specifically where softer ones are not so satisfactory.

Chocolate. I use plain, dark chocolate, not milk chocolate which is too sweet for my taste.

Cocoa. Where listed, cocoa means unsweetened cocoa powder.

Eggs. When using a recipe that includes separated eggs, first beat the whites and then the yolks. This way there is no need to wash the beater in between processes.

There need be no waste if you are just using either the yolks or the whites – store egg-whites in a screw-top jar in the fridge and they will keep for weeks. Use them for Banana Frost and Fire (see page 43) amongst other things. See the index for other ideas.

Egg yolks will keep too, although not for so long. Store them in a small cup closely covered with foil and use them up in quiches, sauces, *crème patissière* or truffles.

Flour. Unless otherwise specified 'flour' means plain flour.

Herbs. As the proud planter of an herb garden I am lucky enough to have access to fresh herbs during much of the year and I use them liberally in all kinds of combinations. However, herbs dry very well, and often are as effective in their bottled guise as the fresh ones. Which herbs you use is a question of taste: there are no hard-and-fast rules about which ones go best with which ingredients: everyone has their own preferences, and it's fun experimenting.

Nuts. I have not always specified which kind of nuts to use since the kind I use varies with what I have in the larder as well as with my mood. The basic range covers walnuts, almonds, hazelnuts and salted peanuts, according to taste.

Oil. A question of taste and mood: I like cooking with a light vegetable oil much of the time, but when the fancy takes me I switch to olive oil – I make all my salad dressings and mayonnaise with it. For deep-frying the light vegetable oil is definitely the best. Vegetable oil can also be used for greasing a cake or loaf tin: smear it around the tin so that the entire surface is covered, and then dust it with flour. To do this, sprinkle a small amount of flour into the tin and knock it around from underneath so that the surface is completely covered. Knock out the residue and the baked cake will come out without a struggle.

Onions. Here is the most incredible hint of all: nobody believes this until they try it, it sounds so improbable:

When you are peeling onions and you don't fancy all that crying, put a metal fork or spoon between your teeth. You may feel – and even look – like Fanny Hill but I defy you to

try it: I can guarantee that you will be tearless at the end of the session.

Stock. I usually have stock in the fridge, made from chicken bones or the bone from a joint: it is such an easy thing to make and always comes in handy. Just cover the bones with cold water and add a peeled onion, dried bay leaves, a bouquet of fresh or dried herbs, a few peppercorns, and salt. Bring to the boil and simmer for several hours. Leave to cool, then strain off into a jug and store in the fridge. It will keep for several days, and also freezes well.

If however you have no stock, stock cubes are an adequate alternative and always handy to have stored in the larder.

Sugar. Unless otherwise specified, sugar means white, granulated, sugar.

Syrup/Treacle. When you are measuring – one of the nastiest, stickiest jobs there is – it is best to weigh the bowl or pan that you will use, then pour in the required quantity of syrup or treacle.

Note on Quantities.
I have not given numbers of servings for every recipe since appetites vary so much, not only between children, but also from day to day: the cook-in-charge will be the best judge of how much the family will or can consume.

Breakfast and Brunch Breaks

For many people the first meal of the day tastes the most delicious. The well-tried breakfast favourites never fail, whether they be croissants, porridge, grilled tomatoes with fried bread, bacon and eggs, or sautéed kidneys with mushrooms. When it comes to brunch, however, the fast has been that much longer, and the appetite is that much more receptive. In addition it is a refreshing break from the usual morning routine (i.e. nobody gets ticked off for getting up late). By mid-morning the resident cook is awake enough to concoct something original for the hungry family – and by that time they tend to be ravenous. These recipes will not fail to make their mouths water.

Greedy Goldilocks' Muesli

This is my own home-made version of a popular stand-by; it is crisp and crunchy and sweet enough not to need any extra sugar added to it at table. I use it in various recipes for biscuits, too.

¾ lb/350 g porridge oats
2 oz/50 g bran
3 oz/75 g barley kernels
a sprinkling of sunflower seeds
a handful of chopped nuts
¼ pint/150 ml vegetable oil
¼ pint/150 ml Golden Syrup (see
    page 15)

Mix all the ingredients together thoroughly. Put the mixture into a large, shallow baking tray and bake at 350°F/180°C/gas 4, turning from time to time until lightly browned. It will take about 20 minutes. When cooked, add a handful of currants. Let cool, then store in airtight jars.

Paddington's Grapefruit

grapefruit
marmalade

Halve some large, ripe grapefruit. Loosen the segments with a serrated knife and spread the tops with good home-made marmalade (see pages 113–15). Put under a hot grill until the marmalade bubbles and serve at once.

Yummy Yogurts

Yogurt is very versatile: there are many ways of inventing your own special flavourings and mixtures to make a refreshing start to the day.

Try adding 2 large tbs muesli (see above) to a 5 fl oz/150 ml carton of plain yogurt, and mix them together in a little bowl.

To flavour and sweeten plain yogurt, add 2 tbs runny honey, or jam (plum, blackcurrant, apricot and strawberry are especially good). Mix it in well and it is ready to eat.

Adding fresh fruit, finely chopped and mixed into yogurt, is also delicious: sliced bananas, chopped pears, fresh blackberries, sliced oranges or mandarin sections, or halved grapes are all excellent. As a variation, you can mix in some barley kernels as well – they add texture and body to the mixture. One of the great favourites in my family is finely chopped (peeled and cored) apple mixed into yogurt, with the addition of muesli or any crispy cereal to give it extra crunch. My favourite combination is grapefruit segments sliced into yogurt: it is refreshing and never fails to wake me up!

Roly Poly Bacon

rashers of bacon   *toothpicks*
bananas   *fried bread*

Cut some bananas into 1 in/2.5 cm chunks and wrap them in rinded, stretched bacon rashers (see Handy Hints on page 12). Secure them with a toothpick and bake at 400°F/200°C/gas 6 for 15–20 minutes until the bacon is crisp. Serve on fried bread.

You can improvise with other fillings too: little rolls of sausagemeat, leftover stuffing, or cockles, for example.

Batman Banana Brunch

bacon
bananas
buttered toast

This has proved to be one of the most popular brunches of all for my family.

Fry the rashers of bacon until crisp, and keep them hot in a low oven. Halve bananas lengthwise and cut them into quarters. Fry in the hot bacon fat until golden all round. Serve immediately, with buttered toast.

Moonshine Mushrooms

Per person:
1 slice of bread   *2 rashers of bacon*
butter   *1 oz/25 g button mushrooms*

Cut off the breadcrusts and butter the slices on one side only. Grill, buttered side up, until a pale golden-brown. Butter the other side and press, with the browned side down, into a square ovenproof dish.

Fry the bacon until crisp and then cook the chopped mushrooms in the fat, with extra butter if necessary, until

they are soft. Place the mushrooms on the toast, cover with the bacon and bake in a hot oven (450°F/230°C/gas 8) for 5 minutes.

Eggs with a Hat

Per person:

1 slice of bread	*1 egg*
vegetable oil	*salt and pepper*

Cut a round out of each slice of bread with a pastry cutter or small glass. Set the slices aside, and fry the circles in oil until golden-brown on both sides. Place on baking tray in a low oven to keep warm.

Begin to fry the remainder of the slices, then break an egg into the hole in the middle and season with salt and pepper. Continue cooking until the bread is golden, then turn carefully with the egg, adding more oil if necessary.

Serve on hot plates with the cut-out rounds on top of the eggs.

Scrimble Scramble

4 *rashers of bacon*
vegetable oil
4 *eggs*

4 *slices of cheddar*
4 *thin slices of onion*
buttered toast

Fry the bacon until it is crisp. Break the eggs into the fat (adding a little oil if necessary) and spread the bacon around the pan, breaking the eggs with a fork. Put the slices of cheese on top and the slices of raw onion on top of that. When the cheese has melted, cut the mixture into 4 and serve on buttered toast. For 4.

Sunrise Surprise

black pudding
1 *egg per person, separated*
milk or cream
salt and pepper
chopped herbs
vegetable oil
bread and butter

This is one of the best brunches there is, in my opinion. It makes a real treat of one of those late, lazy weekend mornings.

Skin and grill thin slices of black pudding until they are crisp on both sides. Drain on kitchen paper, cool and crumble.

Beat the yolks of the eggs with a little milk or cream. Season. Add the crumbled black pudding and some chopped herbs. Fold in the stiffly beaten egg-whites and fry in oil in a heavy pan until the bottom is golden. Keep the heat moderate otherwise the outside of the eggs will burn. Fold the eggs over double and turn out onto a hot dish. Cut into wedges and eat with hot bread and butter.

If you're not feeling energetic enough to do more than simply grill the slices of black pudding until they are crisp, they make a delicious brunch served with hot buttered toast.

Crispy Crackles

These crispy little fish-balls are a real treat: they melt in the mouth and can be guaranteed to vanish as quickly as they are produced. They can be prepared the day before and cooked in no time at all the next morning.

1 small onion, grated	*1 oz/25 g fresh white breadcrumbs*
1 oz/25 g butter	*2 oz/50 g cheese, grated*
1 oz/25 g flour	*a little beaten egg*
¼ pint/150 ml milk	*salt and pepper*
12 oz/350 g white fish, cooked,	*vegetable oil*
boned and flaked	

Gently fry the grated onion in butter for 5 minutes. Add the flour, stir for 2 minutes then gradually stir in the milk. Bring to the boil, stirring all the time, then lower the heat and simmer for 3 minutes. Add the fish, breadcrumbs, cheese, egg, and salt and pepper. Stir thoroughly, let cool, and then chill.

Divide into 12 balls and deep-fry in oil at 390°F/195°C/gas 6 (see page 62) for 3–4 minutes until golden and puffed. Drain on kitchen paper and serve at once.

Super Soups

Beautiful Soup, so rich and green,
Waiting in a hot tureen!
Who for such dainties would not stoop?
Soup of the evening, beautiful soup!
Soup of the evening, beautiful soup!
    Beau-ootiful Soo--oop!
    Beau-ootiful Soo--oop!
Soo--oop of the e--e--evening,
    Beautiful, beautiful soup.
Alice's Adventures in Wonderland by Lewis Carroll

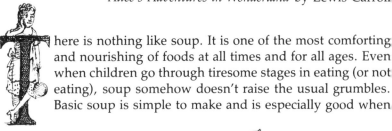 here is nothing like soup. It is one of the most comforting and nourishing of foods at all times and for all ages. Even when children go through tiresome stages in eating (or not eating), soup somehow doesn't raise the usual grumbles. Basic soup is simple to make and is especially good when

made with home-made stock, and in addition there is something about the smell of stock drifting from the kitchen
which is warm and homey. Many of the soups here are
labour-saving and can make quick and substantial meals in
their own right, served with one of the breads on pages
72–3, fresh from the oven with plenty of butter, or with
some of the sandwiches on pages 66–72.

Cheese Soup

1 oz/25 g butter
1 tbs chopped onion
1 tbs flour
½ pint/300 ml stock

½ pint/300 ml milk
¾ lb/350 g cheese, grated
croutons

Gently fry the chopped onion in butter until softened. Stir
in the flour and gradually add the stock and the milk,
stirring until it thickens. Add the grated cheese and simmer
until the cheese melts. Serve with croutons.

Cheese and Onion Soup

2 lb/1 kg onions, thinly sliced
6 oz/175 g butter
1 pint/600 ml stock
2 bread rolls or some French bread,
  sliced

¾ lb/350 g cheese, grated
salt, pepper and nutmeg

Melt the butter, add the onions, and fry in a covered pan
over a very gentle heat until soft. This will take about an
hour. Add the stock and simmer, stirring a few times, until
thoroughly mixed, about 15 minutes. Season to taste. Put
layers of bread and cheese in a casserole and moisten with
the onion mixture. Bake, covered, at 375°F/190°C/gas 5 for
45 minutes and serve hot and thick. This makes a large
quantity.

   As a variation on this soup, to make it even more of a
meal, add lightly boiled flowerets of cauliflower to the
layers of bread and cheese and cook in the same way.

Corn Cauldron

1 tin (¾lb/350g) sweetcorn
½ pint/300ml boiling water
½ pint/300ml milk
1 small onion, sliced
1oz/25g butter
1 heaped tbs flour
salt and pepper

Combine the corn, liquids and onion and simmer over a low heat for 10–15 minutes. Melt the butter, stir in the flour and gradually add the hot corn mixture. Bring to the boil and simmer for a few minutes. Liquidise and season to taste. Thin out with more milk, reheat and serve.

Cottage Pottage

2 bunches watercress
2oz/50g butter
1½ pints/1l stock
salt
4oz/100g cheese, grated

Wash and trim the watercress. Chop it finely and cook in the butter for a few minutes, then add the stock. Bring to the boil, season with a little salt and stir in the cheese. Serve when the cheese has melted. Serves 4.

Spellbound Soup

¾lb/350g potatoes
¾lb/350g sprouts
1½lb/750g leeks
1pint/½l stock
1pint/½l milk
butter and lemon juice
grated Parmesan or other hard
   cheese
salt and pepper

Sauté the washed and chopped vegetables in butter for 10–15 minutes. Add the stock and milk and cook until soft, about 20 minutes. Add the lemon juice and season to taste. Liquidise and serve sprinkled with grated cheese.

Secret Soup

1 tin (8 oz/250 g) baked beans
1½ pints/1 l water
4 slices of onion

3 stalks of celery, chopped
1 tin (8 oz/250 g) tomatoes
½ tsp salt

Bring the baked beans, water, onion and celery to the boil and simmer for ½ hour with ½ tsp salt. Add the tomatoes and liquidise. Season to taste.

Sunset Soup

So straightforward to make, and always popular with children.

leftover cooked carrots
good stock

milk
salt and pepper

Liquidise the carrots in the stock. Heat through and finish with a little milk. Season to taste and serve.

You can also add to it shredded lettuce leaves lightly sautéed in a little butter: it makes a delicious summer starter.

Puss in Boots Soup

1 lb/500 g cooked beetroot,
   chopped
4 stalks celery, sliced

¾ pint/450 ml stock
salt and pepper
double cream

Combine the beetroot with the celery. Simmer for 20 minutes in the stock and liquidise. Season to taste and serve hot with a little cream to finish.

Luscious Lunches

The thing about lunches is that – on holiday at any rate, and when children are very young – they have to happen every day, and the problem is thinking up ideas. The recipes included here are relatively quick and easy to make and provide tasty and satisfying food that children love. Many of them became the classics of my own childhood, and now seem destined to become firm favourites with the next generation.

Tunny Noodle Doodle

8 oz/250 g noodles, cooked
1 tin (7 oz/200 g) tuna
1 tin (10 oz/300 g) condensed
   mushroom soup
½ a tin-full milk

4 oz/100 g frozen peas, or leftover
   sprouts
salt and pepper
grated cheese
dried breadcrumbs

Mix the first five ingredients together, season and put in a greased ovenproof dish. Sprinkle with a mixture of cheese and breadcrumbs and bake at 325°F/170°C/gas 3 for 30 minutes.

This recipe has infinite variations; you can use chopped chicken instead of fish; fresh mushroom sauce (see page 132), béchamel sauce (see page 132) or fairly thick tomato sauce (see page 133) instead of the tinned soup; or try it with sautéed kidneys.

Funtime Fish

8 oz/250 g pasta shells
4 oz/100 g celery, chopped
a little chopped green pepper
(optional)
¾ pint/450 ml tomato purée, made
by liquidising a 1 lb/500 g tin of
tomatoes with salt and pepper

½ tsp Worcester sauce
1 tsp salt
¾ lb/350 g white fish, cooked and
flaked
4 oz/100 g cheese, grated

Cook the pasta as directed on the packet and drain. Combine the rest of the ingredients and fold into the pasta. Pour the mixture into a greased ovenproof dish and bake at 350°F/180°C/gas 4 for 25 minutes.

Hickory Dickory Loaf

1 tin (1 lb/500 g) salmon
4 eggs, whisked

4 oz/100 g melted butter
3 oz/75 g fresh breadcrumbs

Mash the salmon, beat in the whisked eggs and melted butter and stir in the breadcrumbs. Turn into a greased loaf tin and bake standing in a pan of water, at 350°F/180°C/gas 4 for 1 hour. Turn out when cold.

Simple Simon Noodles

8 oz/250 g egg noodles
4 oz/100 g cheese, grated
salt and pepper
1 lb/500 g cooked, sliced chicken
¾ lb/350 g mild mustard sauce (see
page 133)

Cook the noodles. Drain, and stir in the cheese. Season and put in a greased ovenproof dish. Cover with the pieces of chicken and pour the sauce over the top. Bake at 375°F/190°C/gas 5 for 20–30 minutes or until well browned.

Simplicity Chicken

4 chicken joints	1 tin-full milk
butter	1 medium onion, finely chopped
2 tins (10oz/300g each) condensed mushroom soup	

Fry the chicken in butter until golden-brown. Place in the bottom of an ovenproof dish. Mix the soup with the milk over a gentle heat, and add the onion. Pour the mixture over the chicken pieces and bake at 325°F/170°C/gas 3 for about an hour.

For a variation on this dish, replace the mushroom soup with 10oz/300g of freshly made béchamel sauce (see page 132) or tomato sauce (see page 133).

Susan's Lamb Chops

(Serves 4)

2 onions, finely chopped	1 tin (8oz/250g) tomatoes
vegetable oil	¼ pint/150ml stock
4 lamb chops	¼ pint/150ml double cream
salt and pepper	dried breadcrumbs

Fry the onions gently in oil until softened. Season the chops well and sauté until well browned. Put them into an oven-proof dish, cover with the tomatoes and their juices, and add the stock. Heat through in the oven, add the cream, adjust the seasoning and sprinkle with breadcrumbs. Bake for ½ hour at 350°F/180°C/gas 4.

A delicious variation on this theme is to use leeks instead of tomatoes, in which case you need to increase the amount of stock.

Toad in the Hall

oil pastry (see page 136)	1 small onion, chopped
1 lb/500g sausagemeat	water
2 rashers of bacon, chopped	salt and pepper

Make a 10in/25cm pastry case and bake blind. Fry the sausagemeat, crushing it down with a wooden spoon, and add the chopped bacon and onion. Add a little water, season, and simmer for 15 minutes. Put into the pastry case and cover with a lattice of pastry trimmings. Bake at 400°F/200°C/gas 6 for 25–30 minutes or until browned. Serve hot or cold. This quantity goes quite a long way even with the heartiest of appetites.

Toad's Surprise

And his best one: this is extraordinarily delicious for something so easy to prepare.

$\frac{3}{4}$lb/350g sausagemeat $\frac{1}{2}$ an onion, chopped
1 egg   salt and pepper
$\frac{1}{4}$ pint/150ml milk

Line a greased 8in/20cm flan dish with the sausage meat, pressing it out to about $\frac{1}{4}$in/$\frac{1}{2}$cm thick. Beat the egg with the milk, add the onion and season to taste. Pour into the case and bake for 45 minutes at 375°F/190°C/gas 5.

Muppet Meat Loaf

8 oz/250 g fresh breadcrumbs
1½ lb/750 g mince
1 onion, finely chopped
½ tsp salt
1 tsp celery salt
pepper
4 oz/100 g cheese, grated
¼ pint/150 ml tomato juice
2 large or 3 medium eggs

Combine all the ingredients and put into a greased loaf tin. Bake at 350°F/180°C/gas 4 for 1 hour. Turn out when it has cooled a little.

Spanish Meat Balls

2 slices of bread
milk
1 lb/500 g mince
2 eggs
chopped parsley
juice and grated rind of ½ lemon

1 tbs walnuts, pounded
salt and pepper
flour
vegetable oil
boiling water

Cut off the breadcrusts and soak the slices in milk. Mix all the ingredients except the flour together in a bowl and season well. Shape into balls, roll in flour and fry lightly in oil. Put into a deep pan, add boiling water to cover and simmer for 20 minutes. Serve with tomato sauce (see page 133).

Hoppin' Ham Loaf

1 lb/500 g cooked ham, minced
½ pint/300 ml milk
2 oz/50 g bread

chopped parsley, salt, pepper and
mace
1 egg, beaten

Cut off the breadcrusts. Heat the milk to boiling, pour it over the slices of bread and mash the mixture until smooth.

Add the ham and mix well. Season and add the beaten egg. Put into a greased loaf tin and stand in a pan of hot water. Bake at 325°F/170°C/gas 3 for 1 hour. Turn out when cold.

Rodeo Spaghetti

8 oz/250 g pasta shapes
2 onions, sliced
butter
1 lb/500 g mince
¾ pint/450 ml tomato sauce (see page 133)
4 oz/100 g mushrooms
4 oz/100 g Cheddar or Parmesan, grated
salt and pepper

Fry the onions very gently in butter. Increase the heat slightly, add the mince and fry until browned, turning all the time. Add the tomato sauce and the mushrooms and simmer for 15 minutes. Meanwhile, cook the pasta *al dente*. Add the grated cheese to the sauce and season well. When the cheese has melted, mix into the pasta and serve hot.

Spring Ring

This is a delightful diversion into the realms of egg cookery: quick and easy to make and with a taste quite unlike the usual egg dishes, it is a wholesome meal in itself.

6 eggs, separated   *2 oz/50 g mushrooms, sliced*
salt and pepper   *butter*
2 oz/50 g streaky rashers of bacon

Crisp the bacon and fry the mushrooms in butter and set aside. Pour the unbeaten whites into a well-greased oven-proof dish. Place over a pan of boiling water and poach them, stirring, until they begin to set. Beat the yolks, season them, and pour over the whites which should be just firm enough to support them. Keep over the heat until the whites are set. Cool slightly, run a knife around the sides and turn out. Sprinkle the bacon and mushrooms over the top, cut into wedges, and serve.

Another delicious way of serving this is to cover it with a thick onion sauce (see page 133), coat it with grated cheese and brown it under the grill.

Hush Puppy

1 oz/25 g butter
1½ lb/750 g mashed potato
1 egg, beaten
¾ lb/330 g cooked chicken, chopped

¾ pint/450 ml béchamel sauce (see page 132)
chopped parsley

Melt the butter and add to the potatoes. Form into a ring around the edge of a greased shallow ovenproof dish 6 in/15 cm in diameter. Brush with beaten egg and brown in the oven at 375°F/190°C/gas 5 for 20 minutes. Add the chopped chicken to the hot sauce and pour into the centre of the potato ring. Garnish with chopped parsley.

There are endless variations on this theme: cooked fish, mushrooms, ham, hard-boiled eggs etc., can all take the place of chopped chicken in the sauce.

Piggy Potatoes

4 oz/100 g Cheddar, grated
1 lb/500 g potatoes, cooked and sliced

2 eggs
½ pint/300 ml milk
salt and nutmeg

Grease a baking dish, and cover the base of the dish with half the cheese. Cover evenly with the potatoes. Mix the eggs, milk and seasonings and pour over the top. Cover with the rest of the cheese, dot with butter and bake for 45 minutes at 350°F/180°C/gas 4.

Starlight Carrots

4 spring onions, chopped
1½oz/40g butter
10—12 small carrots

salt, pepper and chopped parsley
¼ pint/150ml single cream

Fry the chopped onions in the butter over a gentle heat until soft. Put into an ovenproof dish with the whole, washed carrots and seasonings. Pour the cream over the top and bake, covered, for 45 minutes at 350°F/180°C/gas 4.

Sunset Carrots

1½oz/40g butter
2oz/50g onion, chopped
1lb/500g carrots

1 tsp sugar
salt

Sauté the onions in the butter over a gentle heat to soften. Add the carrots and mix well. Add the sugar, and salt to taste. Cover and bake at 350°F/180°C/gas 4 for 30 minutes.

Fried Cabbage and Nuts

One of the best ways I have yet discovered of getting children to enjoy their greens.

cabbage (or cauliflower, lettuce, spring greens etc.), finely shredded
a mixture of walnuts and raw peanuts, chopped

onion, sliced thinly and shredded
salt and pepper
vegetable oil

Heat some oil in a heavy pan. Place the onion and cabbage in the pan with the chopped nuts. Cover and cook very gently for 10–15 minutes, stirring occasionally. Season with salt and pepper and serve.

Lickety Splits

Lip-licking ways of cooking vegetables.

Lettuce. Cut a lettuce heart into quarters and cook in a little butter over a low heat, closely covered. Shake frequently, then season with salt and pepper and chopped fresh herbs. It is particularly good with Welsh Rarebit.

Peas. Ever tried cooking frozen peas straight from the freezer in a little butter? Toss them until they are heated through but still crisp: they are wonderful.

Cabbage. Deep-fry (see page 62) leftover cooked cabbage in vegetable oil until crisp: it is simply delicious.

Bean Sprouts. Stir-fry lightly in butter until they are hot but still crisp.

Potatoes. Thinly slice raw potatoes and sauté in butter, turning constantly, until the slices are coated. Then leave to cook over a gentle heat, covered, until the bottom is browned and the rest cooked through.

Carrots. How about trying out on the child who emphatically declares that he hates carrots a mixture of potatoes and carrots cooked together and mashed with butter and milk?

Star-Wars Salads

1. Banana slices, nuts, orange wedges and lettuce with mayonnaise.
2. Orange sections, tomato wedges, chopped celery and peanuts in a light mayonnaise.
3. Pineapple chunks, cottage cheese, chopped celery and nuts mixed with a little mayonnaise.
4. Chunks of banana rolled in finely chopped peanuts and served on lettuce. Top with mayonnaise.
5. Tuna, chopped celery and tomato wedges dressed with mayonnaise.
6. Cold diced turkey with peas, celery, walnuts and mayonnaise, served on lettuce.
7. Sardines, hard-boiled eggs, tomatoes and mayonnaise.
8. Cold, cooked pasta mixed with finely chopped vegetables and tossed in vinaigrette.
9. Chopped, cooked potato and hard-boiled egg quarters in vinaigrette.
10. Peeled, grated cucumber dressed with vinaigrette.

Recipes for mayonnaise and vinaigrette are on page 134.

Funny Bunny Salad

Put half a tinned pear, rounded side up, on a bed of shredded lettuce. Insert almonds for ears and carrot rings for the eyes and nose. Use a tiny button mushroom for the tail.

Cheese for Choosey Children

Cheerful Cheese Pudding

6 oz/175 g rice
4 eggs, separated
1 pint/600 ml milk

1 oz/25 g melted butter
4 oz/100 g Cheddar, grated
salt and pepper

Cook the rice. Beat the egg yolks and add them with the milk, butter, and cheese to the cooked rice. Season with salt and pepper. Beat the whites until they are very stiff, fold into the mixture and bake in a greased ovenproof dish for 25 minutes at 350°F/180°C/gas 4.

Crusty Cheese

Cut the crust off of 4 slices of dry bread. Spread the slices with butter, and cut each slice into 8 strips. Put a layer in a greased baking dish and arrange the rest of the strips upright around the sides. Mix, and pour into the centre:

2 eggs, beaten
½ pint/300 ml single cream
1 tsp salt
½ tsp mustard

pepper
8 oz/250 g Cheddar, cut into small
   dice

Bake for 30 minutes at 350°F/180°C/gas 4.

Cheese Crumble

1 onion, chopped
butter
8 oz/250 g mince
8 oz/250 g sausagemeat
½ pint/300 ml stock
salt and pepper
4 tomatoes, sliced
2 oz/50 g mushrooms, sliced

For the topping:
2 oz/50 g butter
4 oz/100 g flour
2 oz/50 g cheese, grated
salt and pepper

Gently fry the onion in butter until it is soft, then increase the heat slightly, add the mince and sausagemeat and fry until browned, stirring well. Add the stock and the seasonings and pour into an ovenproof dish. Cover with the tomato and mushroom slices.

To make the topping, rub the butter into the flour, add the grated cheese and seasonings and sprinkle over the meat mixture. Bake at 375°F/190°C/gas 5 for 35 minutes.

Farmhouse Cheese Flans

¼ *pint/150 ml milk*	1 *egg, separated*
2 *oz/50 g fresh white breadcrumbs*	4 *oz/100 g Cheddar, grated*
1 *oz/25 g butter*	*salt, pepper and mustard.*
oil pastry (see page 136)	

Bring the milk to the boil, stir in the breadcrumbs and butter, and leave to cool. Line some little greased Yorkshire pudding tins with the pastry, pressed out thinly. Sprinkle a little of the cheese in the bottom of each. Beat the yolk and add with the rest of the cheese and seasonings to the breadcrumb mixture. Beat the white stiffly and fold into the mixture. Turn into the pastry cases and bake at 375°F/190°C/gas 5 for 30 minutes. Serve at once.

Puddings

Little Red Riding Pud

8 *oz/250 g red eating apples*
¼ *pint/150 ml double cream*
1½ *oz/40 g icing sugar, sifted*
2 *tbs lemon juice*
a pinch of salt

Grate the apples on a medium grater. Whip the cream with the sifted sugar and salt, and mix in with the apples and lemon juice. Chill, and serve in glasses.

For a tangy flavour, substitute yogurt for the cream.

Gooseberry Grunt

1 lb/500 g gooseberries
4 oz/100 g sugar mixed with a
   pinch of allspice

water
4 oz/100 g Little Miss Muffins
   dough (see page 74)

Wash, top and tail the gooseberries. Roll in the sugar/all-spice mixture and put in a greased baking dish with a little water. Roll out the dough and cover the top of the dish. Bake at 375°F/190°C/gas 5 for 30 minutes. Serve with thick cream or custard.

Jack Horner's Corner

2 eggs
2 oz/50 g sugar
1 oz/25 g flour, sifted

6 oz/175 g currants
sweet pastry (see page 137)

Line an 8 in/20 cm flan dish with the pastry and bake blind. Beat the eggs with the sugar until pale and creamy. Beat in the flour and then mix in the currants. Pour into the pastry case and bake at 350°F/180°C/gas 4 for 40 minutes or until set.

Roly Poly Pudding

chopped fruit, such as pears, apples
   or plums
Little Miss Muffins dough
   (see page 74)
sugar

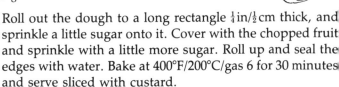

Roll out the dough to a long rectangle ¼ in/½ cm thick, and sprinkle a little sugar onto it. Cover with the chopped fruit and sprinkle with a little more sugar. Roll up and seal the edges with water. Bake at 400°F/200°C/gas 6 for 30 minutes and serve sliced with custard.

Baked Toffee Apples

6 apples, cored
1½oz/40g butter
2 tbs flour

6oz/175g brown sugar
1 tsp vanilla essence

Peel the apples halfway down. Put them into an ovenproof dish, peeled side up.

Melt the butter and stir in the flour. Mix well and add the brown sugar and vanilla. Spread over the apples. Bake at 425°F/220°C/gas 7 for 20–25 minutes or until the apples are soft. Serve hot.

Apple Rumble

2 lb/1 kg apples, cored, peeled and
    sliced
¼ pint/150 ml water
8 oz/250 g Cornflakes

4 oz/100 g butter, melted
6 oz/175 g sugar
a pinch of salt
cinnamon

Arrange the apple slices in a greased ovenproof dish and pour the water over them. Mix the Cornflakes with the butter, sugar and spices and spread over the apples. Bake at 350°F/180°C/gas 4 for 30 minutes or until the crust is golden.

Peach Ice Cream

½ pint/300 ml double cream
1 tin (1 lb/500 g) peaches

Whip the cream. Reserve a few pieces of peach for decoration, then liquidise the rest with half of the juice in the tin. Fold into the whipped cream. Freeze and serve decorated with slices of peach.

This is a wonderful way of using any tinned or fresh fruit. Mangoes, for example, make an exotic and delicious ice cream.

Ice Cream Topping

2 oz/50 g soft brown sugar
1 oz/25 g butter
2 oz/50 g crushed Cornflakes

Melt the sugar and butter together, then add the Corn-flakes. When cold, crumble over ice cream.

Paddington Pie

4 oz/100 g butter   *2 tbs marmalade (see pages 113–1)*
4 oz/100 g icing sugar   *biscuit crust (see page 137)*
3 eggs

Line an 8 in/20 cm greased flan dish with the crust. Cream the butter with the sugar until light. Beat in the eggs and the marmalade and pour into the pastry case. Bake for 1 hour at 325°F/170°C/gas 3.

And finally two winners without which no childhood is complete:

Lovely Lemon Pudding

This is gorgeous; the top is cake-like and spongy, and con cealed underneath is a lovely lemony liquid.

6 oz/175 g sugar   *4 oz/100 g sugar*
4 oz/100 g flour   *rind and juice of 2 lemons*
½ tsp baking powder   *1 oz/25 g butter, melted*
¼ tsp salt   *¾ pint/450 ml milk*
3 eggs, separated

Sift together the sugar, flour, salt and baking powder. Beat the egg-whites until stiff. Then add the sugar, a spoonful at a time. Beat the yolks and add the lemon juice and rind, the melted butter and the milk. Stir into the flour mixture and beat until smooth. Fold in the whites and pour into a large greased ovenproof dish. Set in a pan of hot water and bake for 45 minutes at 350°F/180°C/gas 4. Chill for at least 1 hour.

Upside-down Chocolate Pudding

So-called because the sauce which you pour over the sponge mixture before cooking sinks to the bottom, and the cake rises to the top.

3 oz/75 g self-raising
flour
2 tbs cocoa
a pinch of salt
4 oz/100 g butter
4 oz/100 g caster sugar
2 eggs

For the sauce:
4 oz/100 g soft brown sugar
2 tbs cocoa
½ pint/300 ml hot water

vanilla essence
2 tbs milk

Sift together the flour, cocoa and salt. In a separate bowl, cream the butter and the sugar until light. Mix in the eggs and the vanilla and beat to a cream. Add a little of the sifted flour mixture and then gradually fold in the rest with enough milk to make a medium-soft consistency. Pour into a greased ovenproof dish.

To make the sauce, combine the brown sugar and the cocoa. Stir in the hot water and mix well. Pour over the cake mixture and bake at 375°F/190°C/gas 5 for 40 minutes. Serve hot or cold.

Banana Bonanza

There can be hardly any children who don't like bananas: so
here it is, the Banana Bonanza:

Banana Crunch

6 bananas
juice of ½ lemon
butter

macaroon crumbs
almond flakes
biscuit crumbs

Cut 6 bananas lengthwise and brush them with lemon juice.
Fry them lightly in butter. Arrange them in a greased oven
proof dish and sprinkle with the macaroons, almonds and
biscuit. Dot with butter and bake at 350°F/180°C/gas 4 until
golden.

This is just one of the variations that you can try on the
theme of baked bananas: they are also delicious simply
peeled, sliced thinly and sprinkled with lemon juice and
brown sugar, dotted with butter and baked; or you can use
fresh orange juice, or marinate the slices in fresh lemon juice
and sugar, sauté them in butter and roll them up inside thin
dessert pancakes (see page 135). Serve them hot, sprinkled
with sugar.

Banana Frost and Fire

4 bananas
1 carton (18 fl oz/½ l) vanilla ice
  cream

2 egg-whites
2 oz/50 g sugar

Peel and halve the bananas lengthwise, cut each piece into three, arrange half of the banana pieces on the bottom of a greased baking dish and cover with the ice cream. Place the rest of the bananas on top.

Beat the egg-whites until stiff and beat in the sugar until the mixture is very thick. Pile on top of the dish and bake at 450°F/230°C/gas 8 for 4–5 minutes. Serve immediately.

Banana and Orange Meringue

2 oz/50 g brown sugar
4 bananas
the grated rind and the juice of 1 orange

lemon juice
2 egg-whites
2 oz/50 g caster sugar

Sprinkle half of the brown sugar in the bottom of a greased ovenproof dish. Slice the bananas lengthwise and lay them on top. Sprinkle with the orange rind, orange and lemon juices and remaining sugar.

Beat the egg-whites stiffly, then add the sugar. Continue beating until very thick. Spread on top of the bananas and bake at 325°F/170°C/gas 3 for 25 minutes. Serve hot or cold.

Pooh Bear Pudding

3 bananas
2 oz/50 g walnuts
2 tbs runny honey

For the crumble topping: *2 oz/50 g butter*
2 oz/50 g flour   *2 tbs caster sugar*
1 tsp mixed spice   *2 tbs medium oatmeal*

Peel and slice the bananas. Chop the nuts coarsely, combine with the bananas, and pour the mixture into a greased baking dish. Spoon the honey over the top.

To make the topping, sift the flour with the spice and rub in the butter. Add the sugar and oats and mix in lightly. Sprinkle over the banana mixture and bake at 375°F/190°C/gas 5 for 30 minutes. This makes a fantastic topping: you can use it with all kinds of fruit puddings instead of a conventional crumble mixture.

Desert Dessert

4 bananas   *½ pint/300 ml cream, whipped*
2 oz/50 g sugar   *chopped peanuts*
juice of 1 lemon

Peel the bananas. Sieve them and add the sugar and lemon juice. Heat to boiling point and then chill. Fold in the whipped cream and spoon into glasses. Serve chilled sprinkled with chopped peanuts.

Banana Nutkin

4 slices of bread
4 oz/100 g nuts, chopped
4 bananas
2 oz/50 g sugar
2 tsp lemon rind
2 eggs
¾ pint/450 ml milk
a pinch of grated nutmeg

Cut off the breadcrusts, grease a shallow flan dish and place 2 slices of the bread on the bottom. Sprinkle with half the nuts, cover with the sliced bananas, then sprinkle with 1 oz/25 g sugar and the lemon rind. Cover with the remaining nuts and smooth down the top. Finish with the last two slices of bread.

Beat the eggs with the rest of the sugar, mix in the milk and pour over the bread. Grate a little nutmeg over the top. Bake at 350°F/180°C/gas 4 for 45 minutes. Serve hot.

Banana Ice Cream

¾ pint/450 ml evaporated milk	juice of 1 lemon
2 eggs, separated	a pinch of salt
4 oz/100 g sugar	1 tsp vanilla essence
2 bananas, mashed	

Beat the evaporated milk until thick. Beat the egg yolks with the sugar until thick and beat in the milk. Stir in the bananas, lemon juice and vanilla. Beat the egg-whites, with a pinch of salt, until stiff. Fold into the banana mixture. Freeze.

Banana and Pineapple Cake

For the batter:	¾ cup/250 ml milk
3 oz/75 g butter	1 banana, mashed
5 oz/125 g sugar	
1 egg, beaten	1 tin (4 oz/100 g) pineapple
8 oz/250 g flour	2 oz/50 g butter
2 tsp baking powder	2 oz/50 g brown sugar
salt	2 oz/50 g nuts, chopped

To make the batter, cream the butter and the sugar and add the beaten egg. Sift together the flour, baking powder and a pinch of salt, and add gradually, with the milk, to the butter mixture. Fold in the mashed banana.

Drain the pineapple and crush it. Melt the remaining

butter and pour it into an 8 in/20 cm square baking tin. Sprinkle the brown sugar over it. Add the pineapple and nuts. Pour the batter over the top and bake at 350°F/180°C/gas 4 for 25–30 minutes. Let cool and cut into 9 squares.

Banana Bread

4 oz/100 g butter	*8 oz/250 g flour*
8 oz/250 g caster sugar	*1 tsp bicarbonate of soda*
2 eggs, whisked	*1 tsp salt*
3 bananas, mashed	*2 oz/50 g walnuts, chopped*

Cream the butter and the sugar and gradually beat in the whisked eggs. Add the mashed bananas and mix well. Sift the dry ingredients into the bowl and fold in until well blended. Mix in the nuts and turn into a greased 8 in × 4 in (20 cm × 10 cm) loaf tin. Bake for 1 hour at 350°F/180°C/gas 4.

As a finale to the bonanza, the goodie that no child has yet been known to spurn:

Humpty Dumplings

½ *banana* per person	*Little Miss Muffins dough (see*
lemon juice	*page 74)*
sugar	*milk*

Slice bananas lengthwise and cut slices in half. Marinate them in lemon juice and sugar. When softened, roll each one in a little parcel of thinly-rolled Little Miss Muffins dough. Brush with milk and sprinkle with sugar. Bake at 400°F/200°C/gas 6 for 10 minutes or until golden-brown.

Easy Eats

There are so many occasions when you have to cook on the run – demands are being made on you from all directions, people are in a hurry, things are happening all around you. Don't despair, this section is for you: these ideas can be prepared quickly and easily, yet provide tasty and nourishing snacks. So if you're looking for the easy way out, read on.

Eager Eggs and Fast Fish

Buttercup Scrambles

slices of bread	*eggs*
butter	*grated cheese*
slices of salami cut into strips	*salt and pepper*
celery, finely chopped	

Cut off the crusts from slices of bread, then soak the slices in melted butter. Bake at 400°F/200°C/gas 6 for 10–12 minutes. Sauté the salami and celery in butter, and then scramble some eggs with them. Add some grated cheese, season well and serve on the hot bread.

Farm Fry

4 slices of bacon, finely chopped	*salt and pepper*
4 potatoes, boiled, sliced	*4 oz/100 g cheese, grated*
1 tbs chopped onion	*4 eggs*

Fry the bacon until crisp. Drain off most of the fat and add the potato, chopped onion, salt and pepper. Sauté until the potatoes are golden and softened. Sprinkle the cheese over it all and break the eggs into the pan. Stir until the eggs are set, and serve immediately on hot plates.

The Three Little Piggy Omelettes

The First Little Piggy

Per person: *1 oz/25 g Bel Paese or other soft*
1 small potato   *cheese*
butter   *salt and pepper*
1 oz/25 g ham   *bread*
2 eggs   *green salad*

Cut the potatoes into thin strips and sauté in butter until tender. Cut the ham into strips and sauté in more butter. Beat the eggs, season them and pour into the pan with the ham and potatoes and a little of the cheese. Season to taste. Cook rapidly, and before folding it over cover with the rest of the cheese. Eat off a hot plate with fresh bread and a green salad.

The Second Little Piggy

who was a vegetarian. . .

He had his omelette cooked in olive oil and filled with green peas. He went home very happy.

The Third Little Piggy

Beat and season some eggs and add chopped cooked vegetables, croutons, diced cold chicken, chopped ham or salami, and grated cheese. Heat the pan until it is very hot, melt some butter until it sizzles and cook the omelette rapidly so that it is crisp on the outside and runny inside. Serve immediately on hot plates with fresh bread and butter.

Hide-and-seek Omelette

½ pint/300 ml milk	salt and pepper
2 oz/50 g fresh breadcrumbs	butter
6 eggs, well beaten	4 oz/100 g cheese, grated

Warm the milk, soak the breadcrumbs in it and add the well beaten eggs. Season with salt and pepper to taste. Melt the butter in a frying pan and when it is sizzling pour in the egg mixture. When the bottom begins to set, sprinkle on the grated cheese and when it melts a little, fold it over and cut into 4 portions.

Speedy Sardines

Four ideas for ringing the changes with a tin of sardines.
1. Halve some sardines carefully, dip in seasoned flour, beaten egg and breadcrumbs and fry them in hot oil until crisp and golden. Serve piping hot.
2. Make a Welsh Rarebit and pour it over sardines on toast. Grill until lightly puffed and golden.
3. Put slices of cheese over some sardines in a flat greased ovenproof dish and grill until the cheese bubbles.
4. Mash the sardines with softened butter and lemon juice, season with pepper, put on squares of fried bread. Heat through and serve.

Stuffed Tunny Buns

Mix grated cheese, 2 chopped hard-boiled eggs, 1 small tin (4 oz/100 g) of tuna, ¼ pint/150 ml mayonnaise (see page 134), some chopped onion and pickle. Stuff into 6 hamburger buns and wrap in foil. Bake at 350°F/180°C/gas 4 for 30 minutes.

Viking Fish Dish

¾ lb/350 g white fish, cooked and flaked
1 egg, beaten
1 onion, chopped
1 cauliflower, cooked and separated into flowerets
4 oz/100 g cheese cracker crumbs

¼ pint/150 ml milk
4 oz/100 g Cheddar, grated
salt and pepper

Combine the fish, beaten egg and the onion. Mix well. Add the cauliflower, cracker crumbs and milk. Season and mix well. Put in a greased ovenproof dish and top with the grated cheese. Bake at 325°F/170°C/gas 3 for 30–40 minutes.

Hasty Ham and Speedy Sausages

Ham Patties

The ease and speed with which these patties are made are merely a bonus to a treat which is delicate beyond expectation.

8 oz/250 g ham, minced
2 eggs
2 oz/50 g dried breadcrumbs
Worcester sauce

salt and pepper
milk or water
vegetable oil

Mix all the ingredients together and add enough milk or water to shape into patties. Fry in vegetable oil until golden-brown on both sides. Makes 10.

Ham Swizzle

6 rashers of gammon
6 tomatoes, halved
6 eggs
¼ pint/150 ml single cream

salt and pepper
2 oz/50 g cheese, grated
1 oz/25 g butter
toast

Grill the gammon and the tomatoes and put them in a greased shallow ovenproof dish. Break the eggs in one at a time, spoon over the cream, season with salt and pepper and cover with the grated cheese. Dot with butter and bake at 325°F/170°C/gas 3 for 15–20 minutes or until set. Serve with hot buttered toast.

Crusty Ham

slices of bread
butter
slices of ham

grated cheese
salt and pepper

Cut off the crusts from thin slices of bread, then dip the slices into melted butter. Cut the slices of ham to the same size and make a sandwich. Cut into quarters.

Work to a paste some grated cheese, butter, salt and pepper and shape into small balls. Put one on each quarter and bake at 400°F/200°C/gas 6 for 10 minutes.

Baa Baa Bacon

Per person:
2 rashers bacon, chopped
vegetable oil

2 large spring onions, chopped
1 heaped tbs medium oatmeal
1 egg

Fry the bacon and onion in oil until cooked. Put in the oats and fry together for another 5 minutes and then add the egg. Stir-fry until the egg is set, then season and serve.

Flopsy Frankfurters

Cut a long slit in each frankfurter and tuck into it a long thin slice of cheese. Grill, cheese side up, until the cheese melts.

Sausage Snacks

1. Fry rounds of sausagemeat in a little butter until crisp. Add some more butter to the pan and fry rings of cored, sliced apple until golden on both sides. Serve hot. This is also good with pineapple rings instead of the apple.
2. Dip croquettes of sausagemeat, well seasoned, into beaten egg and then breadcrumbs, and fry them in hot, shallow vegetable oil until browned all over.
3. Wrap rolls of sausagemeat in Little Miss Muffins dough (see page 74) and bake at 400°F/200°C/gas 6 for 25 minutes.
4. Sausage Burgers.

1 onion, chopped	*salt and pepper*
vegetable oil	*1 egg, beaten*
1 lb/500 g sausagemeat	*flour*
2–3 tbs fresh breadcrumbs	*bread rolls, warmed*

Fry the onion in a little oil until soft. Mix with the sausagemeat and breadcrumbs. Season and bind with the egg. Shape into 8 patties, roll in flour and fry on both sides until golden. Serve inside the hot rolls.

Easy Meat

Hickety Pickety Chicken

Put leftover chicken, cut into strips, on a bed of spinach or broccoli, which has been cooked, drained and then sautéed in a little butter. Cover with a little more spinach and top with béchamel sauce (see page 132) and grated cheese. Dot with butter and bake at 400°F/200°C/gas 6 for 15 minutes.

Olé

8 oz /250 g noodles, cooked
1 large onion, chopped
1 lb /500 g mince
salt, pepper
¾ pint /450 ml tomato sauce (see page 133)

1 lb /500 g French or runner beans, cooked and chopped
cheese, grated

Fry the onion and mince in a pan until the meat browns, seasoning well. Then add the sauce and the beans and simmer until well mixed, thinning out with a little water if necessary. In a big greased ovenproof dish alternate layers of noodles and meat, top with a generous layer of cheese and bake at 350°F/180°C/gas 4 for 30 minutes.

As a flavourful alternative to minced beef, try using chopped chicken.

Shepherd's Secret

1 onion, grated
1 lb /500 g mince
cooked leftover vegetables (such as carrots, leeks, broad beans or green beans)

salt and pepper
gravy (or stock thickened with flour)
1 large packet of potato crisps

Mix the onion with the mince. Fry until browned, season
well and add the vegetables with a little gravy to moisten it.
Put in a greased ovenproof dish. Crush the potato crisps,
spread over the top and bake at 400°F/200°C/gas 6 for 10–15
minutes or until browned.

Hasty Haggis

1 onion, finely chopped
vegetable oil
8 oz/250 g mince
8 oz/250 g rashers of bacon,
  chopped
water or tomato juice
salt and pepper
2 oz/50 g medium oatmeal

Fry the onion in a little oil. Add the meat and the chopped
bacon and brown them. Moisten with a little tomato juice or
water, season and scatter on the oatmeal. Simmer for a few
minutes. Serve hot.

Liver with Crispy Bacon

Per person:
2 oz/50 g lamb's liver   butter or oil
seasoned flour   3 rashers of streaky bacon

Cut the lamb's liver into long slivers about ½ in/1 cm thick.
Coat them well with seasoned flour and fry very quickly in
hot butter or oil until crisp on the outside and creamy inside.
Serve with crisped streaky bacon.

Liver Kebabs

Per person:
2 oz/50 g lamb's liver   sage leaves
1 tomato, cut into wedges   salt and pepper
½ onion, cut into wedges   butter

Alternate squares of lamb's liver, wedges of tomato and onion, and sage leaves, on kebab sticks. Season with salt and pepper, brush liberally with melted butter and grill under a high heat, turning until the liver is cooked. Serve with a mild mustard sauce (see page 133), or with beurre noisette (see page 135).

Very Vegetarian

Mushroom Munch

1 lb/500 g potatoes, peeled and
  grated
salt and pepper
butter

¾ pint/400 ml thin béchamel (see
  page 132)
¼ lb/25 g mushrooms, sliced

Sauté the mushrooms in a little butter. Add to the béchamel and mix well. Put the potatoes into a greased ovenproof dish and season well. Pour the mushroom and béchamel mixture over the potatoes. Bake for 1½ hours at 350°F/180°C/gas 4.

Mophead Mushrooms

4 oz/100 g sliced mushrooms
1½ oz/40 g butter
1 tsp grated onion
2 eggs, separated

2 oz/50 g cheese, grated
salt, pepper and cayenne
4 slices of bread

Sauté the mushrooms and onion in the butter. Combine the yolks, cheese and seasonings. Stir in the onion and mushroom mixture, then beat the egg-whites stiffly and fold in. Toast the bread on one side only, butter the other side and heap the mixture on top. Put under a hot grill until puffed and golden.

Topping Tomatoes

4 tomatoes, skinned and sliced
2 oz/50 g mushrooms, sliced
2 oz/50 g fresh breadcrumbs
2 oz/50 g cheese, grated
1 oz/25 g butter
salt and pepper

Grease a baking dish and put in layers of tomatoes, mushrooms, breadcrumbs and cheese, seasoning each one with salt and pepper as you go along. End with a layer of breadcrumbs, dot with butter and bake for 45 minutes at 350°F/180°C/gas 4.

Crisp Tomatoes

Slice some tomatoes and season them well. Dip the slices into medium oatmeal and fry in bacon fat until browned and crisp. They are out of this world.

Crummy Tomatoes

Fry 6 tbs dried breadcrumbs in vegetable oil until golden. Drain on paper. Sprinkle half of them over the bottom of a greased baking dish. Arrange 3 thinly sliced large tomatoes on top, season, and top with the rest of the crumbs. Bake at 400°F/200°C/gas 6 for 15–20 minutes.

Cheesey Tomatoes

Top halved tomatoes with mashed potato, cover with grated cheese and bake at 400°F/200°C/gas 6 until golden and sizzling.

Toadstools

4 eggs, hard-boiled	2 lettuce leaves
¼ pint/150 ml cooked shrimps	2 small red tomatoes
2 tbs mayonnaise (see page 134)	

Cut a slice from the blunt end of each egg and set aside. Remove the yolks, leaving the whites whole. Cut a slice off the other end so that the eggs can stand up. Mash the yolks with a fork, finely chop the shrimps and add with the mayonnaise. Stuff each egg with one quarter of the mixture and place on a lettuce leaf. Cut the tomatoes in half, scoop out the centres and place upside down on top of each egg. Chop the leftover whites and decorate the tomato tops.

Potato and Cheese Puffs

4 oz/100 g cheese, grated	1 onion, chopped
¾ pint/450 ml milk	salt and pepper
1½ lb/750 g mashed potato	2 eggs, separated

Melt the cheese in the milk over low heat. Add the mashed potato, onion, seasonings and egg yolks. Beat the whites stiffly and fold into the mixture. Bake at 400°F/200°F/gas 6 for 20–25 minutes until browned.

Potato Sticks

Mix some leftover mashed potatoes with a little melted butter. Chill. Pat out to ¾in/2cm rectangles and cut into strips. Brush with beaten egg. Sprinkle with sesame seeds, pressing them into each side, place on a baking sheet and bake at 425°F/220°C/gas 7 until crisp and golden, about 20–25 minutes.

Davy Crocket Croquettes

1 lb/500 g cooked potatoes	*beaten egg*
1 oz/25 g butter	*breadcrumbs*
a little milk	*vegetable oil*
salt and pepper	

Mash the potatoes with the butter and milk over gentle heat and season to taste. Chill. Shape into long rolls, dip in the egg and then the breadcrumbs and fry in vegetable oil until golden all over.

For variety, add chopped onion, grated cheese and egg yolk to the potato mixture. Or try chopped parsley and crumbled crisped bacon, or minced ham or chicken.

Cheesey Eats

Moon Munch

The quick answer to cheese on toast, and far more delicious:

Cut some slices of French bread (or rolls) ¼in/½cm thick. Put onto each piece a slice of Bel Paese, Gruyère or other cheese and arrange these open sandwiches, overlapping, in a baking dish. Put in a very hot oven for about 7 minutes.

Juggling Juggins

4 tbs medium oatmeal
4 oz/100 g cheese, grated
1 tin (1 lb/500 g) tomatoes

3–4 tbs milk
salt and pepper

Mix all the ingredients and season well. Bake at 400°F/200°C/gas 6 for 25 minutes. This is the easiest of stand-bys, and delicious.

You can use other vegetables as well, for example marrow, leeks or peas: in which case add twice as much milk.

Gerfuffles

Mix some re-heated macaroni cheese with chopped hard-boiled egg. Shape into burgers and chill. Dip first in beaten egg and then in dried breadcrumbs. Fry in hot vegetable oil until golden all over.

Curly Locks' Cheese

6 new potatoes
2 oz/50 g cheese, grated
1 onion, chopped

1 oz/25 g butter
salt and pepper

Boil the potatoes in their skins, grate them coarsely and mix with the grated cheese. Gently fry the onion in the butter to soften and add to the potato. Press the mixture down well in a greased frying pan and cook over a low heat until a thick brown crust has formed underneath. Sprinkle with more grated cheese and finish under the grill.

Fred's Noodles

8 oz/250 g noodles
3 oz/75 g unsalted butter
Cheddar, grated (or any fairly hard
    cheese)

Cook the noodles, drain, and then add the butter, turning until the pasta is well-coated. Heap onto a platter and sprinkle with the grated cheese. Toss again until the cheese melts and serve immediately.

Cheesey Stirabout

2 oz/50 g cooked lentils　*2 leeks, cooked and chopped*
butter　*Cheddar, grated*
4 rashers of bacon, chopped

Stir the lentils gently in butter over a low heat. Crisp the bacon, warm the leeks in butter, and then stir all together. Sprinkle with cheese and brown under the grill.

Rum Tum Tiddy

6 oz/175 g cheese, grated　*4 eggs, beaten*
4 oz/100 g fresh breadcrumbs　*salt and pepper*
2 oz/50 g butter

Put the cheese, breadcrumbs and butter in a frying pan and stir together over medium heat. Let them all heat through. When the cheese and butter have almost melted, add the well-seasoned, beaten eggs. Stir until puffy and serve with salad.

Cheese Balls

2 egg-whites　*dried breadcrumbs or crushed*
4 oz/100 g cheese, grated　　*cracker crumbs*
just under 2 oz/50 g flour, sifted　*vegetable oil*
salt and pepper

Beat the egg-whites stiffly with a pinch of salt. Add the cheese and flour and season well. Form into balls, roll in breadcrumbs or cracker crumbs and fry in oil until golden-brown. Serve hot. Makes 16.

Cheese Butterflies

6 oz/175 g cheese, grated *4 oz/100 g flour*
4 oz/100 g butter *¼ tsp salt*

Cream the cheese with the butter. Blend in the flour and salt. Pat into a firm ball and chill. Roll out thinly and cut into butterfly shapes with a cutter (or any other pretty shapes you have). Place on a greased baking sheet and chill again. Bake for 7–10 minutes at 400°F/200°C/gas 6. Makes 24.

Cheese Rolls

6 oz/175 g cream cheese *flour*
2 oz/50 g Parmesan, grated *beaten egg*
2 tbs flour *breadcrumbs*
salt, pepper and nutmeg *vegetable oil*
2 eggs

Beat the cream cheese, Parmesan, flour, seasonings and eggs together. Form into small croquettes and chill. Roll first in some extra flour, then in the beaten egg and finally in the breadcrumbs. Fry in hot oil, turning so that they are golden all over and runny inside. Drain on kitchen paper and serve with Chicken Kebabs (see page 121). Makes 12.

Fantastic Fritters

roperly cooked, fritters can make the lightest and cleanest ⟨
meals. It is important to use a very light batter, to fry in ver⟨
hot, clean oil, and then to drain the fritters well on a pape⟨
towel before serving. Eat them as soon as they are cooked
they never keep well for very long. Usually the savour⟨
fritters benefit from a sprinkling of salt, and the sweet one⟨
of sugar. Fritters never fail to delight children and they a⟨
cooked in a matter of moments – and invariably consume⟨
as fast as you can produce them.

To deep-fry:

Heat clean, light vegetable oil to 390°F/196°C in a deep-fry⟨
or heavy deep pan fitted with a basket. For safety's sake it ⟨
better to use a thermometer to be certain not to exceed th⟨
required temperature. Maintain a moderate heat when th⟨
oil is hot enough.

When you are ready to start frying, dip the fritter into th⟨
fat and fry until the batter is golden-brown and puffe⟨
turning if necessary to brown all over. Lift out in the bask⟨
and drain on paper towels.

When the oil has cooled, strain it through a fine sieve t⟨
collect the pieces that have fallen off in the frying. Clean th⟨
pan and store the oil in the covered, cleaned pan, or in a⟨
airtight bottle kept in a dark place.

Fritter Batter

This can be used for both savoury and sweet fritters.

4 oz/100 g plain flour   *¼ pint/150 ml warm water*
a pinch of salt   *1 egg-white*
3 tbs vegetable oil

Sieve the flour with the salt and stir in the oil. Gradually add the water, stirring well until it is thick and cream-like. Let stand in a cool place for 2 hours and then add a little water to thin out.

Beat the egg-white until very stiff and fold it into the batter just before you use it.

Savoury Fritters

With the above batter, all the following can be made into mouth-watering fritters. Serve them sprinkled with salt.

1. Rectangles of Gruyère cheese.
2. Slices of soft cheese such as Bel Paese, rolled up inside slices of ham and secured with a toothpick. Serve with fried parsley.
3. Cooked, flaked fish added to a little very stiff béchamel (see page 132), and chilled before shaping into balls.
4. Chunks of raw or smoked fish.
5. Leftover cooked meats, finely chopped, mixed with a little very stiff béchamel (see page 132) and shaped into croquettes.
6. Slices of sausagemeat, or lightly grilled chipolatas.
7. Strips of ham.
8. Rashers of streaky bacon, stretched (see page 12), rolled up, secured with a wooden toothpick.

9. Sweetcorn added to very thick béchamel (see page 132), bound with egg yolk, and formed into balls.
10. Vegetables such as lightly cooked cauliflower, Brussels sprouts, courgettes, or raw mushrooms. Best of all are slices of cucumber, peeled and dried with a towel: they taste like courgettes and are delicious.

Dessert Fritters

1. Use fruits such as bananas, oranges, peaches or ripe pears. Cook in the same way as the savoury fritters but dust with caster or icing sugar.
2. Jam Fritters: dip spoonsful of the fritter batter into deep, hot oil and fry until golden and puffed. Drain on paper and serve sprinkled with icing sugar and a dollop of your favourite jam in the middle (see Jolly Good Jams pages 113–17).

Five Fantastic Fritters

Ah! Fritters!

Kipper Fritters

Cut off the crusts from some slices of bread. Butter the slices and cut them into fingers. Lay strips of kipper fillets on each one, roll them up and secure each one with a wooden toothpick. Dip in beaten egg and deep-fry until crisp and golden. Drain on paper towels and serve.

Chicken Paper Bags

Sprinkle chunks of raw chicken meat with salt, pepper and lemon juice. Wrap in rice paper to make little parcels and secure with wooden toothpicks. Deep-fry until golden all over, drain on paper towels and serve with a green salad.

You can also make simpler chicken fritters by seasoning

chunks of the raw meat and dipping them in fritter batter, deep-frying and serving with wedges of lemon.

Country Fry

4 lamb's kidneys, finely chopped   1 potato, grated
4 oz/100 g bacon, finely chopped   1 egg, beaten
1 onion, grated   salt, pepper and fried parsley

Mix the kidneys, bacon, onion and potato. Add the beaten egg and seasoning, and drop by the spoonful into hot deep-frying oil. Fry until golden-brown, drain on paper and serve with fried parsley.

Sweetcorn Balls

1 large tin (½lb/250 g) sweetcorn   4 tbs chutney
1 onion, chopped   4 eggs, lightly beaten
4 tbs self-raising flour   salt and pepper

Mix all the ingredients and season well. Scoop into balls with a small spoon and deep-fry in small spoonsful until they are golden-brown and puffed. Drain on kitchen paper and serve.

Little Cheese Parcels

4 oz/100 g flour   1 tbs boiling water
a pinch of salt   ground black pepper
1½ oz/40 g butter   grated Gruyère
2 tsp anchovy essence (optional)

Sift together the flour and salt and rub in the butter. Mix in the anchovy essence with the boiling water to make a stiff dough. Knead and roll out thinly. Cut into 3in/7.5cm squares. Liberally pepper the cheese and place a spoonful on each square. Fold in half to make a triangle and seal the edges with water. Deep-fry until golden. The outside will be crisp and the cheese inside melted.

Smashing Sandwiches

andwiches can be the best or the worst of meals. At best, made with home-made bread, good butter, and an inventive filling, they are unbeatable – and a nutritionist's dream. At worst, pre-sliced plastic bread thinly spread with margarine and sheltering meagre slices of dry and equally plastic ham are allowed to pass under the same name (surely grist to the mill of the Trades' Descriptions Act official).

With a little flair and imagination, sandwiches, hot and cold, can be mouth-watering and satisfying meals in themselves, and are quickly and easily prepared. As a variation on the theme, the so-called Ploughman's Lunch is a wonderful meal and children enjoy it enormously: it is also one that they can help prepare. All you need is fresh bread, good butter, an exciting selection of cheeses and a wide variety of pickles and chutneys. Serve it with sliced raw vegetables such as celery, carrots, mushrooms, cucumber and tomatoes. Try it out as a summer Sunday lunch party: it makes a labour-saving change from the traditional fare.

French Fried Sandwiches

Cut the crusts off slices of bread and spread the slices with butter mixed with a little mustard.

For the filling: mix chopped ham, Gruyère, chicken or corned beef, and make the sandwiches. (Or just make a plain cheese sandwich with Cheddar.) Press them down well and chill.

To fry: dip in beaten egg mixed with a little top of the milk or cream, and fry in vegetable oil until golden-brown on both sides. Serve hot.

Mister Men Sandwiches

Cut off the crusts from 2 slices of bread, and make a cheese and ham sandwich. Fry in vegetable oil until golden-brown on both sides.

Hot Peanut Butter Sandwiches

Cut some thin slices of bread, and remove the crusts. Butter the slices and fill them with home-made peanut butter (see page 117). Bake in a low oven (300°F/150°C/gas 2) for 15 minutes. They are scrumptious: the butter permeates the bread and makes it soft, and the outside remains slightly crisp. As a variation, add a little crisped bacon to the filling.

These peanut butter sandwiches are delicious cold. For Lucy's Special Sandwich, add thinly sliced banana to the filling.

Strammer Max

Fry slices of bread in vegetable oil or butter and cover with a slice of ham and a slice of cheese. Put a fried egg on top and serve with grilled tomato halves.

Jackanapes

Cut some rounds out of slices of bread with a pastry cutter or small glass. Toast the rounds on one side and butter the other side. Stiffly beat some egg-whites and fold in finely grated cheese, chopped green pepper and seasonings. Fold in some crisped bacon, heap onto the buttered side of the bread and grill until golden-brown and set, about 5–8 minutes.

Toasted Sandwiches

Bacon and Cheese

Slice some bread and spread with butter. Sandwich with crisped bacon and grated cheese. Put under a hot grill until toasted on both sides.

Tunny Fish

Toast slices of bread, butter them and sandwich thickly with some tuna mashed with salad cream or mayonnaise (see page 134). Warm through rapidly in a moderate oven and serve.

Other fillings for Toasted Sandwiches

1. Minced ham and mustard.
2. Finely chopped, sautéed kidneys and crumbled, crisped bacon.
3. Crispy bacon and lettuce.
4. Slices of frankfurter and diced pineapple.
5. Chunks of fried fish mixed with scrambled eggs.

Sweet Toasted Sandwiches

Use fillings such as lemon curd, mashed banana, or jam mixed with chopped nuts, and grill the sandwich on both sides until toasted.

For a variation on this theme, try spreading a slice of fresh bread with butter and a thick layer of brown sugar. Grill until the sugar melts.

Cinnamon Toast

This is always a popular treat. Simply sprinkle cinnamon and a little caster sugar (or crunchy brown sugar) onto hot buttered toast.

A more elaborate version is:

Butterscotch Toast

8 slices of bread
2 oz/50 g butter
3 tbs brown sugar

$\frac{1}{2}$ tsp cinnamon
4 bananas

Cream together the butter, sugar and cinnamon. Spread the bread with the mixture, cover with the sliced banana and then with the second slice of buttered bread. Grill until toasted on both sides.

Goodies on Toast

1. Beef dripping (especially the dark brown bit at the bottom).
2. Sardines mashed with lemon juice and chopped celery.
3. Scrambled egg with anchovy or flaked kipper.
4. Apples fried in butter and topped with crisped bacon.
5. Finely sliced kidneys fried in butter with a little mustard.
6. Tuna fish mashed with mayonnaise (see page 134), chopped hard-boiled eggs and capers.
7. Cheese melted with a little butter, milk and pepper and grilled until golden.
8. Grilled mushrooms.
9. Grilled tomatoes.
10. Sardine butter topped with mayonnaise, chopped gherkins and capers.
11. Golden Syrup.

Scandinavian Sandwiches

Make very light toast, or use crispbread, and spread mayonnaise (see page 134) on one side. Top it with:

1. Crisped bacon, lettuce and tomato

or

2. Thin steaks cooked rare, with french onions and melted cheese

or

3. Chopped chicken and watercress.

Zebras

One fun variation on the sandwich theme is to use a slice of white bread for the top and brown bread for the bottom. In the summer, chopped washed chickweed makes a delicious filling. It is very like watercress in taste. An old country favourite is a filling of washed, torn, young dandelion

leaves. Alternatively, make your bi-coloured sandwiches with a filling of chopped hard-boiled eggs and shredded lettuce, mixed with a generous quantity of mayonnaise (see page 134) or salad cream.

This filling is perhaps the most irresistible of all:

Sauté chunks of smoked eel or smoked mackerel in a little butter. Scramble some eggs until creamy, season and add a little cream. Mix with the fish and sandwich between two layers of buttered bread.

Pinwheels

Cut off the crusts from thin slices of bread. Butter the slices and spread with your chosen filling. Roll them up, fasten them with toothpicks and chill.

Pancake Sandwiches

Make a mixture of cooked, chopped chicken, fish or mushrooms, thick mild mustard sauce (see page 133), and a little cream. Make layers with pancakes and cut in wedges to serve. (For pancakes see page 135.)

Cock-eyed Loaf

Mix a tin of sardines with chopped hard-boiled eggs, shredded lettuce and mayonnaise (see page 134). Cut the crusts off a sandwich loaf and slice the bread lengthwise. Butter the slices and sandwich with the filling. Press under a weight and chill. To serve, cover with mayonnaise and cut in vertical slices. Garnish with chopped gherkin.

You can also substitute other fillings of your choice.

Tommy Tucker's Supper

2 oz/50 g butter
2 large tomatoes, fresh or tinned
4 oz/100 g cheese, grated
1 egg, well beaten
salt and pepper

If using fresh tomatoes, scald and peel them. Chop them finely. Melt the butter in a frying pan, add the tomatoes and the cheese. Lastly add the beaten egg and seasonings. Simmer for 2–3 minutes and allow to cool before using as a filling for slices of fresh, buttered bread.

Bread Fingers

Cut off the crusts from slices of bread and cut the slices into long fingers. Spread with butter or garlic butter (see page 135). Place on a baking sheet and bake at 300°F/150°C/gas 2 for 20–30 minutes. They will go with any of the soups on pages 22–5 and are just that bit more original than toast or bread.

Quick Breads

Diddle Diddle Dumpling Bread

8 oz/250 g self-raising flour   *1 tbs milk*
1 level tsp salt   *1 tbs water*
¼ pint/150 ml milk   *poppy seeds*

Sift the flour and salt into a large bowl. Mix quickly to a soft dough with the milk, using a fork. Turn out onto a floured board and knead lightly for a minute or two until the dough is light and smooth. Shape it into a round with your hands and place it on a greased and floured baking sheet. Brush the top with milk and water to give it a nice golden crust. Sprinkle with poppy seeds and bake at 425°F/220°C/gas 7 for 30–35 minutes. Allow to cool down a bit, then eat it warm. It also makes lovely nutty toast.

Emergency Loaf

Handy for when the system fails and you have run out of bread: this can be made in a matter of minutes and is irresistible.

8 oz/250 g flour
1 oz/25 g butter
1 tsp each bicarbonate of soda and
   cream of tartar
¼ pint/150 ml milk

Sift the flour into a bowl and rub in the butter. Then sift in the bicarbonate of soda and the cream of tartar. Mix quickly to a soft dough with the milk. Knead lightly and fry in a heavy, greased pan over a moderate heat until golden-brown on both sides and done through – about 10 minutes. Serve hot and eat it all up – it doesn't improve with keeping.

Topping Teas and Tempting Treats

ea-time is part of the fabric of childhood memories: incomparable smells of fresh scones, warm cookies, and the allure of the chocolate cake which epitomises happiness to the hungry child. Memories of helping to cut out gingerbread men and of first (dreadfully messy) attempts to roll out pastry, of licking the bowl until it is completely clean of cake mixture remain vivid in later life. What comparison can be made between those home-made teas and clinical, shop-bought packets of biscuits, or a Swiss roll off the production line? They are soulless: no warm ovens and drifting, mouth-watering smells . . .

And as for special treats, no childhood is complete without SIN: the seven deadlies are all here in their satanic sugary guise, vindicated slightly by some savoury treats to redress the sticky balance.

Scones and Breads

Little Miss Muffins

These are made with a baking powder dough that melts in the mouth: the recipe provides a versatile stand-by for all kinds of things from sausage rolls (see page 52) to Gooseberry Grunt (see page 38).

The muffins are best eaten the same day, preferably still warm from the oven.

8 oz/250 g flour
4 tsp baking powder
1 tsp salt

1 oz/25 g lard
6 fl oz/200 ml milk

Sift the dry ingredients and lightly rub in the fat. Stir in the milk quickly and knead until light. Roll out on a floured board ¾ in/2 cm thick, and cut into circles with a cutter or small glass. Bake for 10–15 minutes at 450°F/230°C/gas 8, or until risen and golden-brown on top. Makes 12–15.

Cheese Scones

Add 4 oz/100 g grated cheese to the Little Miss Muffins dough before adding the milk. Proceed with the instructions and then cut into triangles. Bake on a greased baking sheet and bake at 450°F/230°C/gas 8 for 15 minutes. Makes 15–18.

Orange Muffins

12 oz/350 g plain flour
2½ tsp baking powder
4 tbs sugar
¾ tsp salt
1 egg

juice of 2 oranges and the rind of 1 orange
4 oz/100 g butter
a little milk

Sift the dry ingredients together into a bowl and make a well in the centre. Beat the egg and add with the orange juice and rind. Melt the butter and mix quickly to a dough with enough milk to thin out. Drop spoonsful into greased muffin tins and bake at 400°F/200°C/gas 6 for 20 minutes. Makes 18.

Beanstalk Buns

2 oz/50 g margarine
7 oz/200 g flour
3 oz/75 g fine oatmeal
1 tsp cream of tartar
½ tsp bicarbonate of soda
2 oz/50 g caster sugar
2 oz/50 g walnut pieces, coarsely
   chopped
milk

Mix the flour and oatmeal and rub in the fat. Add the cream of tartar, bicarbonate of soda and sugar. Stir in the walnuts, then mix to a soft dough with milk. Roll out as for scones, cut into rounds and bake at 375°F/190°C/gas 5 for 10–15 minutes or until lightly browned.

Drop Scones

8 oz/250 g plain flour
½ tsp salt
1 tsp bicarbonate of soda
2 tsp cream of tartar
1 oz/25 g caster sugar
2 eggs
1 tbs Golden Syrup (see page 15)
⅓ pint/200 ml milk

Sift the flour, salt, bicarbonate of soda and cream of tartar into a bowl and add the sugar. Mix and then make a well in the centre. Warm the syrup and milk together, lightly mix the eggs, and pour into the centre of the dry ingredients.

Mix with a wooden spoon until the batter is the consistency of thick cream.

Lightly grease a heavy pan and heat on top of the stove until moderately warm. Drop spoonsful of batter onto the hot surface. Cook until the bubbles begin to rise, then turn over and brown on the other side. Serve immediately with butter. Makes 24.

Contrary Mary Pancakes

4 oz/100 g cream cheese
2 eggs, separated
2 tbs sugar
½ tsp salt

2 oz/50 g flour, sifted
milk
butter

Mash the cream cheese until it is smooth. Add the egg yolks, sugar and salt. Stir in some milk alternately with the flour and mix to a smooth batter. Fold in the stiffly beaten egg-whites.

Heat the butter in a pan until it sizzles. Drop in 1 tbs of the batter and cook on both sides until golden. Spread liberally with butter and eat straight from the pan, sprinkled with sugar. Makes 12 medium-sized pancakes.

Hunt the Nutkin Bread

2 eggs, beaten
4 oz/100 g dark brown sugar
1 lb/500 g flour
4 tsp baking powder

½ tsp salt
1 pint/600 ml milk
6 oz/175 g chopped nuts

Beat the eggs well and stir in the sugar. Sift together into a bowl the flour, baking powder and salt and add to the egg mixture alternately with the milk. Stir in the nuts. Put into 2 greased loaf tins and let stand for 30 minutes. Bake at 350°F/180°C/gas 4 for 40 minutes or until done.

Mud Pie Bread

(otherwise known as Malt Bread . . .)

8 oz/250 g self-raising flour
½ tsp salt
1 oz/25 g brown sugar
2 oz/50 g raisins
1 oz/25 g walnuts
2 tbs black treacle
¼ pint/150 ml plus 2 tbs milk
2 tbs malt extract

Sift together the flour and the salt and stir in the sugar, raisins and walnuts. Warm together the treacle, milk and malt extract until well-blended and pour into the flour mixture. Mix well with a wooden spoon and pour into a greased loaf tin. Bake at 325°F/170°C/gas 3 for 40 minutes. Cool, turn out, wrap in foil or plastic wrap and leave for a day or two before eating.

Gingerbread

4 oz/100 g butter
4 oz/100 g dark brown sugar
2 eggs
10 oz/300 g black treacle (see page 15)
4–6 tbs milk
10 oz/300 g flour
pinch of salt

1 tsp ground ginger
½ tsp mixed spice
½ tsp bicarbonate of soda
2 oz/50 g raisins
rind and juice of 1 orange, grated
2 oz/50 g preserved ginger (optional)

Cream together the butter and the sugar and beat in the eggs. Warm the treacle and milk and add alternately with the sifted dry ingredients; beat thoroughly. Stir in the raisins, orange juice and rind, and ginger if you are using it. The mixture will be very runny. Bake in a greased loaf tin at 310°F/160°C/gas 2/3 for 40–45 minutes, depending on how gooey you want it to be. When cold, turn out and wrap in foil or plastic wrap and eat the next day – or keep it for longer, as it stores very well in the refrigerator.

Individual Cakes

Best Brownies

> 2 eggs
> 4 oz/100 g sugar
> 2½ oz/65 g butter
> 3 heaped tbs cocoa

> 2 oz/50 g flour
> 1 level tsp baking powder
> 4 oz/100 g chopped nuts
> 4 oz/100 g raisins

Beat the eggs and the sugar until thick and pale. Melt the butter and stir in the cocoa. Sift together the flour and the baking powder and mix all the ingredients together. Add the nuts and the raisins. Pour into a greased, square tin and bake at 350°F/180°C/gas 4 for nearly 30 minutes. Cool slightly and cut into squares. Remove from the tin when nearly cold. Makes 12.

Quaker Crunch

> 4 oz/100 g butter
> 4 oz/100 g brown sugar
> 6 oz/175 g porridge oats

Cream together the butter and the sugar until soft, then stir in the oats until well-blended. Spread on a shallow greased baking sheet, pressing down evenly, and bake at 375°F/190°C/gas 5 for 25 minutes. Cut into squares when cool, and then turn out when cold.

Infallible Meringues

Infallible and miraculous: using only one egg-white, this recipe makes 2 baskets or a great pile of individual meringues.

1 egg-white	*2 tbs boiling water*
a pinch of salt	*8 oz/250 g caster sugar*

Lightly beat the egg-white with an electric mixer. Add all the other ingredients and beat over a bowl of hot water until fluffy. Off the heat, beat thoroughly for another 2 minutes. Put in spoonsful on a lightly greased baking sheet, or make two 7 in/18 cm circles and bake for 1 hour at 300°F/150°C/gas 2.

As a variation, add 2 oz/50 g chopped and roasted cobnuts to the mixture.

Biscuit Cake

4 oz/100 g butter	*3 oz/75 g glacé cherries, chopped*
1 tbs Golden Syrup	*2 oz/50 g each chopped nuts and*
8 oz/250 g Digestive (or other)	*sultanas*
biscuit crumbs, crushed	*chocolate*

Melt the butter with the syrup and add the crushed biscuit crumbs, chopped cherries, nuts and sultanas. Press into a greased cake tin to set and pour melted chocolate over the top when cold.

You can use leftover biscuits or muesli (see page 16) for this recipe – they work very well even when they are a bit stale.

Date Squares

8 oz/250 g chopped dates (dried or	*6 oz/175 g butter*
fresh)	*6 oz/175 g demerara sugar*
2 tbs lemon juice	*8 oz/250 g porridge oats*
2 tbs water	*a pinch of salt*

Heat the dates in the lemon juice and water until soft. Heat the butter and the sugar in another pan until the butter has melted. Stir in the oats and salt. Press half the oat mixture over the bottom of a greased 8 in/20 cm square tin. Spread the date mixture over it and finish with another layer of the oats. Press down well and bake at 350°F/180°C/gas 4 for 50–55 minutes or until golden. When cold, remove from the tin and cut into squares.

Date Bites

5 oz/125 g flour
1½ tsp baking powder
¼ tsp salt
2 eggs
2 oz/50 g sugar
4 oz/100 g light brown sugar
1 oz/25 g butter, melted
2 tbs orange juice
8 oz/250 g dried dates
2 oz/50 g walnut pieces, chopped
rind of 1 orange, grated

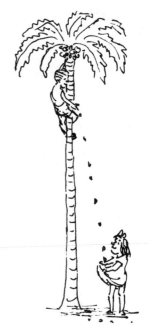

Sift together the flour, baking powder and salt. In a separate bowl, beat the eggs and add both the sugars until the mixture is thick. Add the melted butter and juice, then the fruit, nuts and rind. Sift in the dry ingredients and beat well. Pour into a greased 8 in/ 20 cm square cake tin and bake at 325°F/170°C/gas 3 for 40 minutes. Cool, and cut into little squares. Makes 18.

Biscuits and Cookies

Peanut Biscuits

4 oz/100 g butter   *4 oz/100 g flour*
4 oz/100 g sugar   *4 oz/100 g peanuts, chopped*

Cream together the butter and the sugar, sift in the flour and add the peanuts. Mix to a stiff paste with a little milk if necessary. Form into balls, place on a greased baking sheet and flatten the tops. Cook for 15 minutes at 375°F/190°C/gas 5 until browned. Dust with caster sugar.

Nutteroons

6 oz/175 g flour
2 oz/50 g ground rice or semolina
    flour
2 oz/50 g sugar

1 tsp salt
2 oz/50 g flaked or nibbed almonds
5 oz/125 g butter

Sift the flour and add the other dry ingredients. Work in th
butter until a pliable dough is formed. Knead until smootl
and roll out. Cut into rounds and bake at 350°F/180°C/gas
for 10 minutes or until lightly browned.

Smiley Biscuits

The Nutteroons recipe (above) lends itself beautifully t
making Smiley Biscuits: roll out the dough and cut it int
rounds. Then make smiley faces using chopped walnuts o
currants for the eyes, and cutting a large grin out of th
bottom of the circle.

Sugar Crisps

2 oz/50 g soft butter
2 oz/50 g sugar
2 oz/50 g flour

1 tsp vanilla essence
1–2 tsp milk

Cream together the butter and sugar, sift in the flour, anc
mix. Add the vanilla and the milk and blend until smooth
Then roll little teaspoonsful of the dough into small balls
and put on a greased baking sheet. Flatten the tops and bak
at 350°F/180°C/gas 4 for 10–12 minutes until golden. Cool o
a rack. They turn out lacy, like brandy snaps.

Treacle Biscuits

8 oz/250 g flour
4 oz/100 g caster sugar
3 oz/75 g butter

6 oz/175 g black treacle (see page
    15)

Sift the flour, stir in the sugar and then rub in the butter. Make a well in the centre and pour in the warmed treacle. Beat all together. Place teaspoonsful on a greased baking dish and bake at 300°F/150°C/gas 2 for 30 minutes. They are crisp and crunchy – a treacle treat.

Oatmeal Cookies

4 oz/100 g flour
1 tsp baking powder
¼ tsp salt
4 oz/100 g butter
10 oz/300 g sugar

2 eggs
1 tsp vanilla essence
6 oz/175 g medium oatmeal, or
3 oz/75 g each of fine and medium oatmeal

Sift together the flour, salt and baking powder. Cream together the butter and sugar, beat the eggs and add alternately with the flour to the creamed butter, mixing well. Beat in the vanilla and the oatmeal. Chill. Roll into little balls and sprinkle with sugar, put on a greased baking sheet and flatten the tops. Bake at 350°F/180°C/gas 4 for 15 minutes.

Ginger Cookies

1 tbs bicarbonate of soda
1 tbs hot water
6 oz/175 g butter
10 oz/300 g brown sugar

2 eggs
10 oz/300 g flour
4 tbs ground ginger
salt

Dissolve the bicarbonate of soda in the water. Cream the fat with the sugar, beat in the eggs and the soda. Sift together the flour, ginger and salt and beat into the mixture a little at a time. Drop teaspoonsful of the mixture 2in/5cm apart onto a greased baking sheet and bake for 20 minutes at 350°F/180°C/gas 4.

Maryland Cookies

4oz/100g butter	4oz/100g flour
1oz/25g sugar	¼ tsp salt
2oz/50g brown sugar	½ tsp bicarbonate of soda
¼ tsp vanilla essence	2oz/50g chopped nuts
1 egg	4oz/100g chocolate

Cream the butter with the sugars and vanilla until light and fluffy. Add the egg and beat well. Sift together the flour, salt and soda, and add them to the mixture. Stir in the nuts and the chocolate chopped up to the size of small peas. Drop teaspoonsful onto a greased baking sheet and cook at 375°F/190°C/gas 5 for 10–15 minutes or until golden.

Cakes

Hedgehog

A party centrepiece, fun to make and a great character who will amuse the kids.

6 oz/175 g butter	*a little milk*
6 oz/175 g icing sugar	*grated chocolate*
2 egg yolks	*a few toasted almonds and small*
6 oz/175 g chocolate, melted	*round sweets*
1 box sponge fingers	

Cream the butter with the sugar, and add the egg yolks one at a time, adding the melted chocolate as you go. Mix thoroughly. Dip the sponge fingers quickly into the cold milk to soften them. Make a flat round shape on a plate with the chocolate cream, cover with biscuits and continue making these layers until the biscuits are used up, saving enough of the chocolate mixture to mould around the outside to make a hedgehog shape. Cover liberally with grated chocolate. Cut the toasted almonds into strips and stick them in the hedgehog's back. Use little round sweets for its eyes and mouth.

Scottish Chocolate Cake

The lightest and most infallible chocolate cake I have ever made.

6 oz/175 g flour	*1 heaped tsp baking powder*
2–3 tbs cocoa	*5 oz/125 g sugar*
2 large tbs black treacle	*5 fl oz milk*
2 eggs	*5 fl oz vegetable oil*
1 heaped tsp bicarbonate of soda	

Beat all the ingredients together in a bowl. Pour into 2 greased and floured 8 in/20 cm cake tins. Bake at

325°F/170°C/gas 3 for 35–45 minutes or until done. Sandwich with jam when cold.

Ice with chocolate spread if you want it to look like paten
leather: the bonus with this is that it takes about one minut
to do. If you feel more energetic or if the kids have scoffed al
the chocolate spread, try:

Diana's Chocolate Icing

3 tbs Golden Syrup
3 oz/75 g butter
3 tbs cocoa

Melt the syrup with the butter and beat in the cocoa with a
fork. Cool a little, beating well, and when thick pour ove
the cake and allow to set.

Queen Mum's Cake

Pour 1 breakfast cup of boiling water over 8 oz/250 g chop
ped, dried dates. Add 1 tsp bicarbonate of soda and allow to
stand while mixing:

3 oz/75 g butter   *8 oz/250 g sugar*
10 oz/300 g flour   *2 oz/50 g walnuts, chopped*
½ tsp salt   *1 beaten egg*

Add to the date mixture and pour into a greased and floured cake tin. Bake for 35 minutes at 350°F/180°C/gas 4 or until done. Keep for a day or two – it improves with keeping. Ice with:

Fudge Icing

4 oz/100 g brown sugar
1 oz/25 g butter

2 tbs top of the milk (or single cream)

Melt all the ingredients over a gentle heat and then boil for 2–3 minutes. Remove from the heat and beat well until it begins to thicken. Pour over the cake immediately and sprinkle with chopped nuts.

Apple Cake

The recipe for this unbeatable apple cake was given to me by a friend in the village, whose house is always filled with the smells of fresh baking. It is delicious – moist but light, and just as good hot with custard for pudding, as warm at teatime or cold the next day (if there is any left). Keep it wrapped in plastic wrap and it will stay moist.

12 oz/350 g self-raising flour
a pinch of salt
8 oz/250 g butter
6 oz/175 g sugar

4 oz/100 g sultanas
1 lb/500 g unpeeled apples, cored and diced
3 eggs

Sift together the flour and salt and rub in the butter. Stir in the sugar, sultanas, and apples. Break in the eggs and stir in with a spoon. Do not beat. Bake in a large greased cake tin at 350°F/180°C/gas 4 for 1 hour and 15 minutes. Dredge with caster sugar and serve warm from the oven.

Treacle Cake

4 oz/100 g butter
8 oz/250 g self-raising flour
1 tbs sugar
dried fruit (optional)
4 oz/100 g black treacle (see page
  15)

¼ pint/150 ml milk
1 tsp bicarbonate of soda
1 egg, beaten

Rub the butter into the flour, add the sugar and dried fruit if
you are using it. Warm the treacle and the milk together and
add the bicarbonate of soda. Mix together with the beaten
egg and add to the dry ingredients. Beat thoroughly. Bake at
350°F/180°C/gas 4 for ¾ hour or until done.

Julie's Quick Sponge

4 oz/100 g sugar
4 oz/100 g self-raising flour

1 tsp bicarbonate of soda
2 eggs

Beat all the ingredients together for 5 minutes. Pour into 2
greased sandwich tins and bake for about 15 minutes at
350°F/180°C/gas 4. Sandwich with jam or cream and dust
with icing sugar.

Devil's Food Cake

4 oz/100 g butter
6 oz/175 g sugar
2 eggs
8 oz/250 g flour

1½ oz/40 g cocoa
½ tsp bicarbonate of soda
½ cup strong coffee
1 tsp vanilla essence

Cream the butter until light and add the sugar gradually,
beating until fluffy. Add the eggs and beat thoroughly.
Measure the flour and the cocoa and sift together. Dissolve
the bicarbonate of soda in 2 tbs coffee and add to the rest of
the coffee. Mix together the dry ingredients, the butter
mixture and the coffee and beat until well-blended. Add the
vanilla and pour into a greased cake tin. Bake at

350°F/180°C/gas 4 until done, about 20–25 minutes. Serve covered with sifted icing sugar.

Angel Cake

3 oz/75 g flour	¼ tsp salt
2 tsp cream of tartar	1 tbs lemon juice
6 oz/175 g sugar	1 tsp vanilla essence
6 egg-whites	

Sift the flour. Add half the cream of tartar and sift again. Sift the sugar and set aside. Beat the egg-whites until they form soft peaks. Add the salt and the rest of the cream of tartar to the egg-whites. Add the sugar 2 tbs at a time, and then the lemon juice and the vanilla. Fold in the flour 2 tbs at a time. Bake in a well-greased and floured tube pan or large cake tin at 375°F/190°C/gas 5 for 20 minutes, and then at 325°F /170°C/gas 3 for a further 20 minutes. Remove from the oven, leave to cool for 10 minutes and then turn out.

Now for some treats, starting with:

Four Special Drinks

John Verney's Apple Juice

Simply chop up apples coarsely, removing the worst of the rotten parts but any old windfalls will do. Cover with water in a large pan and simmer until the fruit is soft and pulpy. Strain through a linen tea-towel or jelly bag for several hours or overnight. Add sugar to taste while it is still warm, to give it a chance to dissolve. Squeeze the bag from time to time to get all the juices out. Bottle and store in screw-top bottles. Dilute if necessary with soda water. If placed in the refrigerator the juice will last for a few days.

Marjorie's Orange Juice

2 oranges	*12 oz/350 g sugar*
1½ pints/750 ml water	*1 level tsp citric acid*

Peel the oranges, making sure to remove all of the white pith. Liquidise the pulp and peel and strain. Boil the sugar and water for 5 minutes. Pour the hot syrup onto the oranges, add the citric acid and bottle. It will keep for several weeks in the refrigerator.

Raspberry Cordial

Simmer some raspberries with a little water until they are mushy. Liquidise them, then sieve to separate the pips from the pulp. Sweeten to taste and dilute with water until it is the right drinking consistency.

Frothy Milk Shake

Per person:	*½ pint/300 ml milk*
1 ripe banana	*1 tbs ice cream*

Cut the bananas up and liquidise with the milk. Pour over the ice cream and serve in tall glasses.

Savoury Treats

Fried Cheese

Cut slices of soft cheese (Bel Paese is best) ¼ in/½ cm thick. Dip in flour, beaten egg and breadcrumbs and fry in hot vegetable oil. Drain on paper and serve at once. (Edam and Cheddar work quite well, but are not so creamy inside.)

Toasted Cheese Chunks

Cut cheese of any sort into 1 in/2 cm cubes, stick on the end
of a toasting fork and hold in the flame of a wood fire until
the edges sizzle and the inside is creamy.

Potato Crisps

Peel some potatoes and slice them very thinly – as thin as
paper. (One way to do this is to use the cucumber-slicer on
the grater.) Dry them on a paper towel and deep-fry them
(see page 62) in very hot vegetable oil. Drain on kitchen
paper and serve sprinkled with salt. They keep very well in
airtight jars.

Crisplets

Peel some potatoes and grate them on the coarse side of the
cheese grater. Deep-fry (see p 62) in very hot vegetable oil
(400°F/200°C) until golden and crisp.

Deep-Fried Rice

Deep-fry (see page 62) leftover cooked rice until golden-
brown and crisp. Drain on kitchen paper, sprinkle with salt
and serve as a snack.

Sunflower Seeds

Fry sunflower seeds in vegetable oil until browned all over,
tossing them as they cook. Drain on kitchen paper, sprinkle
with salt and serve when they are cool.

Peanut Straws

3 oz/75 g butter　　　　　　　*salt and pepper*
3 oz/75 g flour　　　　　　　*salted peanuts*
3 oz/75 g cheese, grated

Sift the flour, rub in the butter and add the cheese with the seasonings. Knead to a paste and roll out thinly. Put the nuts in the blender and chop briefly. Press them into the pastry, then cut into long straws and bake at 350°F/ 180°C/gas 4 for 10 minutes or until crisp.

Onion Whirls

Roll out Little Miss Muffins dough (see page 74) into a rectangle ¼in/½cm thick. Spread with finely chopped onion and scatter a few sesame seeds over the top. Roll up, brush with beaten egg after cutting into ¾in/1.5cm slices. Sprinkle with more seeds and bake for 15 minutes at 450°F/230°C/ gas 8, or until done.

Sweet Treats

Yums

Melt some cooking chocolate with a little butter over hot water. Coarsely chop some glacé cherries and stir them into the chocolate. Place teaspoonsful on rice paper to set.

For variety, you can add chopped nuts, but I think they are best simply with cherries.

Truffles

4 oz/100 g chocolate　　　　　*2 egg yolks*
1 oz/25 g butter　　　　　　　*cocoa or powdered drinking*
1½ tbs icing sugar　　　　　　*chocolate*

Melt the chocolate over boiling water and add the butter and the sugar. Stir until the sugar has dissolved. Remove from the heat and stir in the yolks one at a time. Cool for 12 hours, then shape into balls and roll in the cocoa or chocolate powder, whichever you prefer.

Chocolate Orange Rings

oranges *water*
sugar (2 oz/50 g per orange) *cooking chocolate*

Peel the oranges and cut into thin slices. Make a syrup by adding a little water to the sugar and boiling it rapidly until it is thick and forms a thread when it trickles off the spoon. Poach the oranges in the syrup and drain them. When cool, dip them in melted chocolate and put on greaseproof paper to set. Store between layers of greaseproof paper in an airtight tin.

Ride-A-Choc Horse

Cut 2 bananas into ½ in/1 cm lengths. Dip in melted chocolate and roll in very finely chopped nuts. Leave to set.

Marshmallow Roll

2 oz/50 g chocolate *1 packet (4 oz/100 g) marshmallows*
2 oz/50 g butter *aluminium foil*
2 oz/50 g icing sugar

Melt the chocolate and the butter over hot water. Cool a little and add the icing sugar. Cut the marshmallows into quarters with a wet knife and fold them in. Spread on a sheet of foil and roll it up to set in a sausage shape. Wrap with foil and chill. Serve cut in slices.

Toasted Marshmallows

If you're lucky enough to have a wood fire in the house, put each marshmallow on the end of a toasting fork and cook in the flames very briefly so that the outside is browned and the inside creamy.

Peanut Brittle

¼ pint/150 ml Golden Syrup (see page 15)
8 oz/250 g sugar
¼ pint/150 ml water

8 oz/250 g salted peanuts
1 oz/25 g butter
½ tsp lemon juice

Heat the syrup, sugar and water until boiling, then cook to 300°F/150°C/gas 2 and add the nuts with the butter and lemon juice. Pour into a greased tin and let cool. Break into pieces when cold.

Ice Cream Treats

Butterscotch Sundae

4 oz/100 g dark brown sugar
¼ pint/150 ml Golden Syrup (see page 15)

½ tsp salt
1 oz/25 g butter
1 tsp vanilla essence

Heat the sugar and the syrup for 10 minutes. Add the rest of the ingredients and stir well. Pour over vanilla ice cream.

Knickerbocker Glory

3 different colour jellies
ice cream

sliced bananas, peaches, grapes etc.

Place tablespoons of the jellies alternately with the ice cream in a glass, then alternate layers of fruit and ice cream to the top of the glass. Finish with a swirl of whipped cream.

Icebergs

Put scoops of ice cream into glasses and cover with chopped nuts – a mixture of walnuts, hazelnuts and almonds is best if you have them all. Garnish your iceberg with a sprig of mint.

Chopped nuts are always scrumptious on ice cream: try chopped peanuts on chocolate ice cream. Another good thing is liquidised tinned peaches poured over ice cream in tall glasses.

Flowerpots

In the summer when the garden is full of flowers, fill some decorated pots with ice cream, smooth down the top and cover with grated chocolate. Pick some flowers, wrap the stems in foil so that they are sealed, and set them in little bunches in the pots. They look as if they are growing out of earth.

Easy Ice Cream

¼ pint/150 ml double cream
1½ oz/40 g icing sugar, sifted

2 tsp vanilla essence
2 egg-whites

Whip the cream with the sifted sugar until it is thick, then
flavour with the vanilla. Beat the egg-whites until very stiff
and fold them into the cream. Put into a container, cover
and freeze.

Two variations that are very good: add chopped salted
peanuts or crushed biscuit crumbs to the cream before folding in the egg-whites.

Ice Cream Christmas Log

1 lb/500 g vanilla ice cream   *cooking chocolate*
1 lb/500 g chocolate ice cream,
  slightly softened

Turn out the vanilla ice cream on a tray and cover with all
the chocolate ice cream. Re-freeze. Melt the chocolate over
hot water and pour it over the top, making patterns. Decorate with chopped nuts, raisins and glacé fruits and return
to the freezer.

Yogurt Ice Cream

Fold into some plain yogurt honey to taste, some chopped
nuts and raisins. Cover and freeze. Yogurt ice cream is also
lovely with a little caster sugar added to it before freezing.

And to go on top of any of these ice cream treats:

Chocolate Sauce

½ pint/300 ml boiling water   *2 oz/50 g cocoa*
8 oz/250 g sugar   *1 tsp vanilla essence*
a pinch of salt

Mix together all the ingredients except the vanilla and stir
over a moderate heat until smooth. Cook for 10 minutes and
flavour with the vanilla. Store in an airtight jar. You can also
serve it with other puddings – fruit, cakes, etc.

Scrumptious Suppers

uppertime – and back to the problem of What To Have. The ideas here range from satisfying rice and pasta dishes through simple fish and sausage dishes to more elegant chicken meals, rounded off with some scrumptious puddings to send the family contentedly to bed. The end of another cooking day at last . . .

Risottos

Great favourites with both children and adults, and they are of course a wonderful way of using leftovers. The secret of a successful risotto is to sauté whatever ingredients you choose – fish, ham, chicken, or vegetables (whatever is around, in short) – with chopped onion and bacon for quite a while in vegetable oil or butter. Then stir in the rice and let it absorb the fat and the juices. Cook gently, stirring constantly, for 5–10 minutes, then gradually add the stock or water, adding more as it is absorbed by the rice. Season to taste, and when the rice is cooked through, serve with grated cheese.

The other classic way of using rice is in kedgeree. Recipes for this well-known dish usually call for smoked haddock, but why not use tuna, kippers, or fresh white fish?

One particularly delicious and comforting rice dish is:

Rice with Cheese

Grease a baking dish. Cook 2oz/50g rice per person and then drain it well. Cover the bottom of the greased dish with a layer of rice dotted with butter and covered with slices of cheese (allow 2oz/50g per person). Continue with a layer of rice, and so on until all the rice is used. Finish with a layer of cheese, then cover with breadcrumbs and bake at 350°F/180°/gas 4 for 25 minutes.

To make a more complete supper dish, add chopped ham, chicken or hard-boiled eggs to the layers. It is also very good layered with braised lettuce, or very thinly sliced cooked Brussels sprouts.

Pasta Dishes

If pasta is a favourite with your child or children, there are infinite variations on the theme. One of my favourite ways is to cook noodles *al dente*, add chopped ham, grated cheese and raw eggs and toss over a moderate heat until the eggs are lightly set. On the same lines, try it with mushrooms, peas and eggs and serve sprinkled with grated Parmesan. The variations are infinite and can be left to the imagination of any enthusiastic cook.

Here is one macaroni dish that has proved particularly successful:

Cauliflower Gratinata

6oz/175g macaroni
a large cauliflower
¾ pint/450ml béchamel (see page 132)

4oz/100g cheese, grated
4 tomatoes, sliced

Cook the macaroni and boil the cauliflower until tender. Drain and cut into flowerets. Add the cheese to the béchamel. Combine half the sauce with the macaroni and place it in the bottom of a greased baking dish. Arrange the tomato slices around the edge of the dish and pile the cauliflower in the centre. Spoon over the rest of the sauce. Top with more cheese and bake at 425°F/220°C/gas 7 for 30 minutes. Serve at once.

Fish Dishes

Lazy Layers

Easy to cook and not very difficult to eat either . . .

4 oz/100 g breadcrumbs, toasted
1 lb/500 g cooked fish
1 pint/600 ml sauce à la crème (see page 132)
3 hard-boiled eggs, sliced

Grease an ovenproof dish and line with half of the breadcrumbs. Add the fish to the cream sauce and make alternate layers of the fish sauce and sliced eggs. Cover with the rest of the breadcrumbs and bake at 375°F/190°C/gas 5 until the top is brown, about 20–25 minutes.

Igloo Fish

8 oz/250 g cooked flaked fish   3 egg-whites
¼ pint/150 ml béchamel (see page   1½oz/40 g Parmesan
    132)

Heat the béchamel sauce and mix with the fish. Put in the bottom of a soufflé dish. Beat the whites until stiff and fold in the cheese. Spread over the fish and bake at 450°F/230°C/gas 8 until browned, about 10 minutes.

Funtime Fish Flan

oil pastry (see page 136)   gherkins, mushrooms and
1 lb/500 g cooked flaked fish   tomatoes
¼ pint/150 ml mayonnaise (see page
    134)

Line a 10 in/25 cm flan dish with oil pastry and bake blind. Mix the fish with the mayonnaise. Chop the gherkins finely and mix in with the finely sliced raw mushrooms. Put into the pastry case and decorate with the thinly sliced tomatoes.

As a variation, you could try this with chicken instead of fish.

Meat Dishes

Toads in Cheesey Holes

So much tastier than their ordinary holes . . .

For the batter:
4 oz/100 g flour, sifted
½ tsp salt
2 eggs
¾ pint/450 ml milk and
    water mixed
3 oz/75 g cheese, grated
1½ lb/750 g chipolatas

To make the batter, beat the eggs well and stir in the sifted flour and salt. Gradually stir in the liquid until it becomes creamy, then add the cheese.

Fry or grill the sausages until they are well browned and put them in a shallow greased ovenproof dish. Pour the batter over them and bake at 400°F/200°C/gas 6 until crisp and golden, 30–35 minutes.

Mole in the Hole

Make the batter as for the Toads (see above), and pour over meatballs in a shallow greased ovenproof dish. Bake as above.

Roly Poly Pancakes

Roll up a slice of ham in a pancake (see page 135) and warm through in a moderate oven. Make a béchamel sauce (see page 132) and add mustard, Parmesan and a little cream and pour over the pancake before serving.

Jumping Jehosophat

4 potatoes, peeled and sliced	salt and pepper
1 onion, sliced	milk
6 oz/175 g cooked ham, sliced	butter

Grease an ovenproof dish and make alternate layers of potato, onion and ham, seasoning each layer with salt and pepper as you go. Repeat until the dish is full. Pour in milk until the dish is three-quarters full, dot with butter and bake at 350°F/180°C/gas 4 for $1\frac{1}{2}$ hours.

Pig in the Middle

1 lb/500 g carrots, cooked and
  mashed
2 tsp grated onion
1 oz/25 g butter, melted
2 eggs, well beaten
1 tbs flour

2 oz/50 g cheese, grated
¼ pint/150 ml top of the milk or
  single cream
1 oz/25 g fresh breadcrumbs
salt and pepper

Mix all the ingredients and put into a greased ring-mould.
Bake at 350°F/180°C/gas 4 for 20–30 minutes or until set.
 Fill the middle with creamed peas, chicken, ham or tuna
whatever takes your fancy.

Pork and Apple Parcels

4 pork chops
4 large slices of peeled and cored
  apple

juice of 1 orange

Remove the rind from the chops and fry the chops quickly t
brown them. Season, and place on a square of foil. Put
slice of cored apple over the top of each chop. Moisten wit

the orange juice and wrap up securely. Bake for 45 minutes at 375°F/190°C/gas 5.

You can use lamb chops instead, seasoning them with thyme or rosemary.

Easy Meat Loaf

2 lb/1 kg mince
1 egg, lightly beaten
2 tsp salt
½ pint/300 ml stock

4 oz/100 g fresh breadcrumbs
1 oz/25 g dried onion soup
streaky bacon

Mix all the ingredients, except the bacon, and pat into a greased loaf tin. Cover the top with bacon and bake at 350°F/180°C/gas 4 for 1 hour. Serve hot with tomato sauce (see page 133), or cold with chutney.

And now for three chicken dishes:

Chuckling Chicken

The reason he's chuckling is that he knows how good he is . . .

4 boned chicken breasts
lemon juice and oil
3 tbs flour seasoned with
*   salt and pepper*
2 oz/50 g Parmesan, grated
butter
8 oz/250 g rice
4 oz/100 g button mushrooms
2 tomatoes, sliced

Sprinkle chicken with the lemon juice and oil and leave to marinate for a while. Coat the chicken pieces with the seasoned flour and roll in the Parmesan to make quite a thick coating. Fry them in butter, turning until the chicken is cooked. Cook the rice at the same time and butter it lightly. Place in a shallow dish and arrange the chicken around the edge. Fry the sliced tomatoes and the mushrooms, put in the middle and serve.

Chicken Loaf

8 oz/250 g cooked, chopped chicken
2 oz/50 g fresh breadcrumbs
½ pint/300 ml milk
2 eggs
salt, pepper
Worcester sauce
lemon juice
2 stalks celery, chopped

Mix all the ingredients and put into a greased loaf tin. Set in a pan of boiling water and bake at 325°F/170°C/gas 3 for 40 minutes or until firm. Allow to stand for 15 minutes before turning out. Serve hot or cold.

Chicken Roll

6 oz/175 g Little Miss Muffins
dough (see page 74)
8 oz/250 g chopped, cooked chicken
½ onion, chopped
a little gravy or single cream
salt and pepper

Mix the chicken and onion with enough gravy or cream to moisten it, and season to taste. Roll out the dough into a rectangle and put the mixture in the middle. Wet the edges and roll it up, seal the ends securely and place with the fold underneath in a greased ovenproof dish. Bake at 425°F/220°C/gas 7 for 20–30 minutes or until well browned. Cut into slices and serve with gravy, tomato sauce (see page 133) or mushroom sauce (see page 132).

And for afters?

Queen of Hearts Tart

sweet pastry (see page 137)
2 large pears, peeled and sliced
1 egg and 1 egg yolk
1½ oz/40 g sugar
1 tbs cornflour
¼ pint/150 ml single cream
2 tsp vanilla essence

Line an 8in/20cm flan case with sweet pastry and bake blind. Arrange the pears over the cooled pastry. Beat the eggs, sugar, cornflour, vanilla and cream and pour over the fruit. Bake at 375°F/190°C/gas 5 for 25 minutes or until puffed and golden. Serve hot or cold.

Peach Crunch

For the topping:

4 oz/250 g medium oatmeal	1 egg, beaten
6 oz/175 g brown sugar	½ tsp salt
½ pint/300 ml vegetable oil	1 large tin (1 lb/500 g) peaches

Mix the oatmeal, sugar and oil and leave to stand for a few hours. Then mix in the eggs and salt and put into a large square greased baking tin. Bake at 350°F/180°C/gas 4 for 30–40 minutes or until crisp. Let cool.

Break up the topping and sprinkle it over the fruit in an ovenproof dish. Bake at 350°F/180°C/gas 4 for 20 minutes.

You can pre-cook this topping and store it in airtight jars, broken into pieces. It is irresistible eaten as flapjacks: cook in a greased 10in/25cm square shallow tin, mark into squares and turn out when cold: it is deliciously light and crunchy.

Pears with Chocolate Sauce

Peel some pears and cut them into quarters. Sauté them in butter until lightly browned and serve with chocolate sauce (see page 96).

Dragon Pie

In a greased ovenproof dish make layers of apricot jam and sliced apple rings (sprinkle them with sugar as you go along if the apples are very sour). Top with a thick layer of Digestive or other biscuit crumbs. Dot with butter and bake at 350°F/180°C/gas 4 for 30 minutes.

The central heating has broken loose!

Apricot Charlie

1 lb/500 g ripe apricots (or greengages), chopped
½ pint/300 ml double cream

4 oz/100 g peanut brittle (see page 94)

Whip the cream and fold in the chopped apricots. Chill. Crush the brittle with a rolling pin and sprinkle over the top.

Fruit Stirabout

4 oz/100 g flour
a pinch of salt
2 eggs, separated
½ pint/300 ml milk

1 oz/25 g sugar
¾ lb/350 g strawberries or raspberries
1 oz/25 g butter

Sift the flour and the salt into a bowl and make a well in the centre. Put the yolks into the well and draw in the flour, mixing to a thick paste. Stir in the milk gradually to make a smooth batter, and beat until all the milk is used up. Stir in the sugar and add the fruit. Heat the butter in a shallow ovenproof dish in the oven until it sizzles. Whisk the whites until they are stiff, fold them into the batter, then pour it into the prepared dish. Bake for 30 minutes at 375°F/190°C/gas 5 until risen and browned.

Miss Piggy's Pud

8 oz/250 g fresh breadcrumbs
2 oz/50 g butter
1½ lb/750 g mixed fresh fruit, e.g.
  plums, bananas, pears (peeled if
  necessary)
sugar, nutmeg and lemon juice

Mix the breadcrumbs with the melted butter and cover the bottom of a large ovenproof dish with some of the mixture. Cover with a layer of the sliced fruit and sprinkle with sugar, nutmeg and lemon. Repeat the layers, ending with the last of the crumbs. Bake for 40 minutes at 350°F/180°C/gas 4.

Lemon Crumb Pie

2 eggs, separated   *a pinch of salt*
the grated rind and juice of a lemon   *biscuit crust (see page 137)*
1 tin (7 oz/200 g) condensed milk

Line an 8 in/20 cm flan dish with biscuit crust. Beat the yolks until thick, stir in the grated rind and juice of the lemon and then the condensed milk and salt. Beat the whites until stiff and fold them into the lemon mixture. Pour into the biscuit shell and bake for 40 minutes at 325°F/170°C/gas 3. Serve cold.

Beanfeasts

Beans (pulses or legumes) come inescapably under the heading of Comforting Food. Their texture, taste and smell are entirely individual and delicate; even their colours are aesthetically pleasing – earthy, and glowing with a feeling of Nature.

It is hard to undersing their virtues – they are highly nutritious, and as valuable as most meats in terms of protein and vitamin content, at a fraction of the price. Although the smells of cooking pulses linger appetisingly around the kitchen, the famous Pease Porridge and similar soups are not so popular with children as the lighter bean recipes I have included here. Many of them contain cheese, fish or butter – indeed the pulses benefit from being treated rather like pasta – which enriches them in moisture as well as flavour. The mung beans and green flageolets cook in a relatively short time and do not require overnight soaking, a true bonus to the busy cook.

Mung Tuna

4 oz/100 g rice or noodles per person 1 tin (7 oz/200 g) tuna
8 oz/250 g mung beans   cheese, grated

Cook the rice until tender. Cook the beans at the same time – they need to simmer for 20–30 minutes. Flake the fish and add with the cooked beans to the rice or pasta. Put in a greased ovenproof dish, cover with grated cheese and bake at 350°F/180°C/gas 4 for 20 minutes.

Alternatively, heat through under the grill. You can try serving this with a cheese sauce. It is also good cold, with mayonnaise (see page 134)

Rumpelstiltskin Ragoo

6 oz/175 g green flageolets
2 baked mackerel, skinned, boned
    and flaked
4 oz/100 g Cheddar, grated
2 oz/50 g butter
dried breadcrumbs
salt and pepper

Cook the beans until tender, about ¾ hour. Drain and season, and add to the fish. Mix in the cheese and half the butter and put in a greased ovenproof dish. Sprinkle with breadcrumbs and dot with the rest of the butter. Bake at 400°F/200°C/gas 6 for 25 minutes.

Lentil Kedgeree

⅔ green lentils to ⅓ rice
butter
salt and pepper

smoked haddock or kippers, cooked
    and flaked
hard-boiled eggs, halved

Soak the lentils for several hours, then cook them together with the rice for 30–45 minutes. Drain and add a knob of butter and seasonings. Add the flaked fish and hard-boiled eggs, and heat through. It is delicious.

For a change try it with sautéed kidneys instead of fish.

Fuzzy Bear's Beans

bacon
mushrooms, chopped
green flageolets

butter
cheese, grated
salt and pepper

Crisp some bacon pieces in their own fat and then cook some chopped mushrooms gently in the pan. Add to some cooked green flageolets with plenty of butter and grated cheese. Season and heat through.

Pixie Peas

8 oz/250 g split peas	*4 oz/100 g cooked ham, chopped*
1 pint/600 ml water	*3 oz/75 g cheese, grated*
8 oz/250 g rice or noodles	*salt and pepper*

Soak the peas for several hours. Then cover them with the water, bring to the boil and simmer for 30–40 minutes until soft. Cook the rice or noodles in salted water until done. Chop the ham, mix all the ingredients together and season well.

Pease Pudding

1 lb/500 g split peas	*2 egg yolks, beaten*
1 onion	*1 oz/25 g butter*
1 carrot	*salt and pepper*
1 turnip	*sausages and bacon*
1 stalk of celery	

Soak the peas for several hours. Then cook them with the vegetables until tender, about 45 minutes, adding more boiling water as the peas soak up the liquid. When they are

quite soft, liquidise them. Stir in the egg yolks and butter, and season to taste. Put in a greased pudding bowl, cover with foil and steam over hot water for 35–45 minutes or until firm and done through. Turn out into a dish and serve with sausages and bacon.

Pease Fritters

pease pudding (see above)	*dried breadcrumbs*
chopped onion	*beaten egg*
egg yolk	*vegetable oil*

Add to leftover pease pudding (if there is any . . .) some chopped onion, egg yolk and enough breadcrumbs to make a firm consistency. Shape into patties, brush with beaten egg and dip in breadcrumbs. Fry in vegetable oil until golden brown.

Thunder and Lightning

chick peas	*salt and pepper*
olive oil	*cooked pasta*
garlic	*Parmesan, grated*

Soak some chick peas for several hours, drain them and cook in fresh water until tender, about 35–40 minutes. Mix well with olive oil, garlic, salt and pepper. Toss into the cooked pasta – noodles, spaghetti or pasta shapes – and serve hot with grated Parmesan.

Mushrooms on Mars

8 oz/250 g green flageolets	*¼ pint/150 ml béchamel (see page 132)*
vegetable oil	
lemon juice	*1 oz/25 g cheese, grated*
salt and pepper	*1 oz/25 g dried breadcrumbs*
8 oz/250 g mushrooms	

Cook the flageolets for about 40 minutes, drain and dress with the oil and lemon juice, and season to taste. Put in the bottom of a greased ovenproof dish.

Separate the mushroom caps from the stems. Cook the caps in a little oil. Chop the stalks, add them to the béchamel, and pour the mixture over the beans. Arrange the caps, underside up, over the top and sprinkle them with grated cheese and breadcrumbs. Bake at 350°F/180°C/gas 4 for 15–20 minutes.

Green Gratin

Mix some cooked mung beans with cooked fresh peas in a béchamel sauce (see page 132). Sprinkle liberally with grated cheese and heat through in a moderate oven.

Purées

Any of the pulses (soaked, if necessary) cooked until tender and then liquidised with a little of their liquid are excellent cold with olive oil, lemon juice, garlic, salt and pepper.

Hot purées with a little cream added to them make a tasty base for poached eggs, or a good side vegetable garnished with chopped spring onions, sautéed mushrooms or crisped bacon.

Beansprouts

"It's only a bean!"

Use these uncooked in salads (particularly good with Chinese cabbage); or steam them briefly over hot water and serve with butter; or stir-fry them with a little melted butter.

Jolly Good Jams

o home is completely home without a jam cupboard full of good things. There is nothing like the smell of strawberry jam cooking after an afternoon spent picking them in the sun, or the autumnal smell of simmering blackberries after a walk along the hedgerows. Certainly no shop-bought jam is remotely comparable to your own home-made version.

I have included here just a few of my favourites – the jams that have proved the most popular with my family and friends, and which are particularly easy to make.

Oranges and Lemons Marmalade

12 oranges
6 lemons
water

½ tsp bicarbonate of soda
6 lb/3 kg sugar

Squeeze the juice from the fruit and bring it to the boil with the pips. Strain it. Discard the pulp, then slice all the peel, measure it and add twice the volume in water. Add the juice and the soda. Simmer for 1½ hours until the pulp is tender and the quantity well reduced. Add the sugar, stir until dissolved and then boil to setting point. Pot and seal. Makes 10 lb/5 kg.

Sunshine Marmalade

So called not only because it is full of citrus fruits, but also because, by dint of mincing the peel, it is beautifully easy to make.

3 oranges	*5 pints / 3 litres water*
3 grapefruit	*6 lb/3 kg sugar*
3 lemons	

Extract the juice from the fruit, discard the pulp, then put all the peel through a coarse mincer. There will be about 1 pint / 600 ml juice, so add this to the fruit with the water and the sugar, and cook together for about 1½ hours, stirring frequently, until setting point is reached. Makes 9 lb/4½ kg.

Pear Marmalade

2 lb/1 kg ripe pears	*1 lemon*
2 oranges	*1½ lb/750 g sugar*

Wash, core and slice the pears very thinly. Wash the oranges and lemon, remove the ends, then cut them into quarters and slice thinly, removing the pips. Place all the fruit in a pan with the sugar and a little water, and stir

thoroughly. Bring to the boil and simmer until setting point is reached. Pot and seal. Makes 4 lb/2 kg.

Pear, Orange and Walnut Jam

This is the best jam in the world.

2 oranges, washed but unpeeled	*1 lb/500 g sultanas or seeded raisins*
3 lb/1½ kg pears, peeled and cored	*½ pint/300 ml water*
3 lb/1½ kg sugar	*6 oz/175 g walnuts, halved*

Chop the oranges finely. Cut the pears into quarters and slice them thinly. Mix the fruits with the sugar, sultanas and water. Simmer for 1½ hours. Add the halved walnuts and cook for a further 15 minutes, then pot and seal. Makes 5 lb/2½ kg.

Pineapple Jam

This is easy and convenient to make, and the result is rather exotic. Eat it quickly – it doesn't keep for very long.

1 lb/500 g tinned pineapple
¾ lb/350 g sugar

Chop the fruit finely and mix with the sugar and a little of the juice from the tin. Dissolve over a low heat, then bring to the boil and cook to setting point. Pot and seal. Makes 2 lb / 1 kg.

As a variation, make Apricot and Pineapple Jam, using equal quantities of fruit.

Marrow and Pineapple Jam

This is even more delicious than Pineapple Jam: it has a magical texture and is a marvellous way of using up the annual surplus of marrows.

6 lb/3 kg marrow, peeled and seeded　6 lb/3 kg sugar
1 tin (1 lb/500 g) pineapple　　　stem ginger (optional)

Cut the marrow into small cubes, dice the pineapple, and arrange in alternate layers with the sugar. Leave overnight to extract the juice. Add the ginger if you are using it. Boil until setting point is reached, then pot and seal. Makes 10 lbs/5 kg.

Pear Honey

2 lb/1 kg pears, peeled and cored
1 lb/500 g tinned pineapple
1½ lb/750 g sugar

Slice the pears and dice the pineapple. Add the sugar and a little juice from the tin and cook until setting point is reached. Pot and seal. Makes 4 lb/2 kg.

Angels' Hair

Don't tell the kids, but this is carrot jam. See if they guess!

1 lemon　　　　　　　　　*1 lb/500 g sugar*
1 lb/500 g carrots　　　　　*¼ pint/150 ml water*

Extract the juice from the lemon and discard the pulp. Thinly peel the lemon and shred the peel. Peel the carrots and grate them on a coarse grater. Put them with the lemon peel, juice, sugar and water into a heavy pan. Boil to setting point which will be about 200°F/100°C. Pot and seal. Makes 2 lb/1 kg.

Lemon Curd

I've had so many failures with lemon curd that I nearly gave up trying, but then I discovered this method and I have never looked back.

1 lemon　　　　　　　　　*1 oz/25 g butter*
4 oz/100 g caster sugar　　　*1 egg, well beaten*

Put the grated rind and juice of the lemon into a double boiler with the sugar. When dissolved, add the butter and the egg. Stir until thick, then pour into a clean jar and cover. Keeps in a cool place for several weeks. Makes 8oz/250g.

Peanut Butter

This is so unlike the commercial variety that you would find it hard to guess that they were related. Home-made peanut butter is crunchy, delectable, irresistible.

Melt some butter and liquidise with an equal weight of peanuts. The longer you liquidise the smoother it will be. Season to taste with salt and store in airtight jars.

Candlelight Cuddles

hen my little girl was five years old she discovered the romance of eating supper by candlelight. At first it was a secret between the two of us, and there was no question of a candlelight cuddle if visitors were there (that changed after a while but it was a touching start). Part of the ritual was turning off all the lights in the house and then, under careful supervision, she lit the candles herself. We would sit in the half-light eating especially chosen goodies while she attempted rather sweetly to make grown-up conversation. Such was the influence of candlelight on her!

Candlelight makes any meal a special occasion and without a doubt throws a defiant gesture at our interminable winters: many of the recipes here are for comforting food, and perhaps a new tradition of Candlelight Cuddles could help obliterate awareness of the dark world outside during those long, cold months.

Cheddar Fondue

2–3 tbs cornflour
1 tsp dry mustard

pepper
½ pint/300 ml dry cider

Blend the dry ingredients to a smooth cream with a little of the cider and set aside.

1 oz/25 g butter
1 lb/500 g Cheddar, grated

fresh vegetables, sliced
bread

Melt the butter in the fondue pot, add the cheese and the remaining cider. Heat gently and stir until smooth. Add the flour mixture, turn up the heat a little and stir until it thickens. Let it bubble gently while you dip in, using fondue forks, slices of raw celery, carrot, sliced mushrooms, cucumber, and small cubes of fresh bread.

Starlight Eggs

lettuce, shredded
semi-hard-boiled eggs, halved
béchamel sauce (see page 132)
chives, chopped
fried breadcrumbs

Cover the bottom of a greased ovenproof dish with the shredded lettuce. Place the eggs over the lettuce. Make the béchamel with as much cream as you can spare and add masses of chopped chives. Pour over the top and heat through in the oven at 375°F/190°C/gas 5 for 10–15 minutes. Serve sprinkled with fried breadcrumbs.

Three Soufflés

For the soufflé base:
2 oz/50 g butter
1½ oz/40 g flour
½ pint/300 ml hot milk
salt and pepper
4 eggs, separated

Melt the butter, stir in the flour and let simmer for a minute or two. Add the milk gradually, stirring all the time until the base thickens. Season well with salt and pepper and then, off the heat, stir in the well-beaten egg yolks. Then add the selected flavourings (see below). Whisk the whites until they form very stiff peaks, and fold carefully into the base. Bake at 400°F/200°C/gas 6 for 25–30 minutes until risen and set but still a little runny in the middle.

Ham and Lettuce Soufflé

Add to the base 3 oz/75 g minced ham and a shredded lettuce heart braised in a little butter and water.

Leek Soufflé

Add to the base 4 oz/100 g sliced, cooked leeks, and 2 skinned and chopped tomatoes. Add a pinch of nutmeg to the seasoning.

Turkey and Orange Soufflé

Add to the base 4 oz/100 g minced, cooked turkey and ½ tsp grated orange rind. Sprinkle more rind over the top before serving.

Baby Pizzas

For the dough:	1 egg
1½ oz/40 g butter	*½ oz/12 g dried yeast (or 1 oz/25 g*
6 oz/175 g plain flour, sifted	*fresh yeast)*
a pinch of salt	*warm water*

Rub the butter into the flour and add the salt. Make a well in the centre and put in the egg and the yeast dissolved in a very little warm water. Mix well and knead to a smooth dough. Put in a floured bowl, cover with a cloth and leave to rise for 2 hours.

For the filling:	*butter*
vegetable oil	*soft cheese, sliced*
tomatoes, chopped	

Knock back the risen dough and form into lots of little rounds. Allow to rise a second time, about 20 minutes, in a warm spot. Deep-fry (see page 62) in hot oil until golden and puffed, drain well on kitchen paper and put in the middle a hot mixture of fresh skinned tomatoes chopped and cooked in butter. Top with slices of soft cheese, such as Mozzarella or Bel Paese, and melt it under the grill.

Roger's Chicken

A marvellous way of cooking because the rice absorbs all the juices from the chicken and mushrooms as it cooks itself.

4 chicken joints
flour seasoned with
  salt and pepper
vegetable oil
8 oz/250 g rice
½ onion, grated
4 oz/100 g mushrooms, sliced
2 oz/50 g butter
1 pint/600 ml stock

Dust the chicken with seasoned flour and brown in a little oil. Meanwhile put the rice and some salt and pepper in a greased casserole and sprinkle in the grated onion. Sauté the mushrooms in the butter and add, with their cooking juices, to the casserole. Arrange the chicken over the top, pour the stock in and dot with butter. Cover with foil and bake at 350°F/180°C/gas 4 for 1 hour.

Chicken Kebabs

chicken breasts   *mushrooms*
salt and pepper   *vegetable oil*

Cut raw chicken breast meat into chunks. Cut some mushrooms into wedges and impale them alternately with the chicken on kebab sticks. Season well and brush with oil. Grill under a high heat, turning and basting frequently with the oil until the meat is lightly cooked – it is delicious a tiny bit underdone so that it is just pink in the middle. Serve with beurre noisette (see page 135).

Pixie Pineapple Chicken

chicken joints   butter
salt and pepper   tinned pineapple

Season the chicken well, dot with butter, and bake a
375°F/190°C/gas 5 for 20–25 minutes, basting often with
pineapple juice. Serve with chunks of pineapple fried in
butter.

Chicken Wiggle Flan

8 oz/250 g cooked chicken   salt and pepper
oil pastry (see page 136)   2 eggs
1 small onion, chopped   ⅜ pint/200 ml milk
butter   2 oz/50 g cheese, grated
¾ lb/350 g leeks, cooked and sliced

Line a 10 in/25 cm flan dish with oil pastry and bake blind
Slice the chicken and arrange it over the bottom of the
pastry case. Soften the onion in a little butter and stir in the
leeks. Season and place over the chicken. Beat the eggs with
the milk and half of the grated cheese, and season well.
Pour over the top, sprinkle with the rest of the cheese and
bake at 375°F/190°C/gas 5 for 35–40 minutes.

Henny Penny

chicken breasts   soft cheese
butter   mushrooms, sliced
ham

Sauté slices of chicken breast in butter for 5–8 minutes
turning until golden. Cover with a slice of ham and a slice of
cheese and cover the pan. Cook until the cheese has melted
and garnish with cooked, sliced mushrooms.

Goosey Gander Pie

oil pastry case, baked blind (see
   page 136)
1 large onion, finely chopped

6 oz/175 g cheese, grated
salt and pepper

Fill the centre of the pastry with the onion and cover with grated cheese. Season and bake at 400°F/200°C/gas 6 for 30 minutes.

Colourful Pie

8 oz/250 g chipolatas
2 oz/50 g butter
1 onion, chopped
1 lb/500 g leeks, blanched in
   boiling water

4 oz/100 g cheese, grated
salt and pepper
4 tomatoes
oil pastry case, baked blind (see
   page 136)

Fry the chipolatas lightly and cut them in half. Melt the butter and sauté the onion. Slice the leeks and add to the onion with ½ the cheese and the seasoning. Put into the pastry case and lay the sausages on top. Cover with the sliced tomatoes and sprinkle with the rest of the grated cheese. Bake at 350°F/180°C/gas 4 for 15 minutes.

Beef Cornwheels

1½ lb/750 g mince
salt, pepper and thyme
4 oz/100 g cheese cracker crumbs
1 onion, finely chopped

¼ pint/150 ml milk
1 tin (4 oz/250 g) sweetcorn,
   drained
4 oz/100 g Cheddar, grated

Combine the meat, seasoning, crumbs, onion and milk. Lay on foil and pat out to a 12 in/30 cm square. Combine the corn and the cheese and spread over the meat. Roll up like a Swiss roll, wrap the foil around it, and seal the edges. Put on a rack in a roasting pan and bake at 350°F/180°C/gas 4 for 30 minutes. Serve in slices, either hot or cold.

Pork with Prawns

1 lb/500 g fillet pork	*8 oz/250 g mushrooms, sliced*
salt and pepper	*½ pint/300 ml double cream*
butter	*8 oz/250 g prawns*

Cut the pork into thick slices, season and sauté in butter for about 20 minutes until cooked through. Meanwhile sauté the mushrooms very quickly in butter so that they are still crisp, and add to the cooked pork in the pan. Add the cream, heat through and adjust the seasoning. Add the prawns, and serve with rice.

Barbecue Spare Ribs

1 lb/500 g spare ribs of pork　　　*salt*

Cut the ribs into individual pieces and season with salt. Roast at 400°F/200°C/gas 6, for 1 hour. Meanwhile prepare the sauce.

For the sauce:	
1 tbs tomato purée	*1 tbs vinegar*
4 tbs soy sauce	*½ tsp Worcester sauce*
4 tbs water	*2 tsp French mustard*
1 tbs dark brown sugar	*salt and pepper*

Combine all the ingredients in a saucepan and simmer, stirring, for several minutes until well mixed. Baste the roasting ribs often with the sauce for the last 20 minutes of cooking time, and serve with crispy noodles (below).

Crispy Noodles

egg noodles   *salt*
vegetable oil

Cook the noodles until they are soft and drain them. Dry on a towel. Fry them in a shallow pan in hot oil, stirring them around until they are golden. Dry on kitchen paper and sprinkle with salt before serving.

Liver Slivers

4 slices of lamb's liver   *¼ pint/150 ml stock*
4 slices ham   *salt and pepper*
butter   *buttered rice*
2 carrots, thinly sliced crosswise *grilled tomatoes*

Slice the liver very thinly and season well. Put on top of slices of ham and roll up with the ham on the outside. Secure with a toothpick and fry very lightly in butter with the carrots. Add the stock, cover the pan and simmer very gently for 15 minutes. Serve with buttered rice and grilled tomato halves.

Funny Fish

1 onion, chopped
butter
¾ lb/350 g cooked fish, flaked
4 oz/100 g cooked rice
½ pint/300 ml béchamel sauce (see
   page 132)
single cream
8 oz/250 g lettuce, shredded
4 oz/100 g peas
salt and pepper

Sauté the onion in butter over a gentle heat until softened. Mix the fish and rice in a bowl. Add the onions and béchamel and thin out with cream. Sauté the lettuce briefly in the onion pan in a little butter and water; cook the peas until tender and add both to the mixture. Season to taste. Pour into an ovenproof dish and bake at 375°F/190°C/gas 5 for 25 minutes.

And now for a potato section:

Grated Potato Cake

1 lb/500 g potatoes, peeled and   *2 oz/50 g butter*
   grated   *salt and pepper*

Soak the potatoes in cold water, drain and dry them on a towel. Melt the butter in a heavy pan and add the potatoes. Turn until they are covered with butter, and as they begin to soften season them well. Cook, covered, over the lowest possible heat, well pressed down in the pan for about 45 minutes or until browned underneath. Turn out on a hot plate and serve.

Potato Bo Peep

1½ lb/750 g potatoes, boiled   *butter*
milk

Mash the potatoes (with not too much milk and butter). Reserve ⅓ of the potatoes, and spread the rest around the edge of a large baking dish to make a border.

For the filling: *pepper*
½ pint/300 ml double cream   *diced ham*
crushed garlic   *diced cheese*

Heat the cream until it is thick and add some crushed garlic, pepper, diced ham and cheese (Gruyère is best). Put it into the potato ring and refrigerate for a while. Cover with the remaining potato and cook at 400°F/200°C/gas 6 for nearly an hour.

Potato Pancakes

3 potatoes, grated   *1 tsp salt*
2 tbs dry breadcrumbs   *1 small onion, grated*
2 tbs double cream   *vegetable oil*
2 eggs, lightly beaten

Mix all of the ingredients. Stir well and drop spoonsful into hot oil and cook until they are crisp and done through. Turn them to brown on the other side – allow about 5 minutes on each side. These are lovely with grilled or roast chicken.

Pippa's Potatoes

Thinly slice enough potatoes and onions for the helpings required. Cook gently in lots of butter, turning often until well softened. Break one egg per person over the top and put under the grill until set.

Cassy's Potatoes

Slice some cooked potatoes. Put in a baking dish with some good olive oil and soft crumbly cheese such as Wensleydale or Cheshire. Season and put in a hot oven until it sizzles.

Puppy Dog Potatoes

Peel some potatoes and cut them into small cubes. Toss them in butter, season and add chopped parsley and cook until softened. Beat the yolks of 2 eggs with some fresh cream and pour over the potatoes, heating through until lightly cooked. Serve at once.

Puddings

Polar Bear Pudding

1½lb/750g mixed fresh fruit, chopped
4oz/100g packet marshmallows
4 tsp lemon juice
hot water

2 egg-whites
salt
1oz/25g caster sugar
1lb/500g vanilla ice cream

Put the fruit in the bottom of a greased baking dish. Melt the marshmallows with the lemon juice over hot water and leave to cool. Beat the egg-whites with the salt until stiff, then beat in the sugar until very firm. Fold in the marshmallow mixture. Cover the fruit with slices of ice cream, then with the meringue mixture, and bake at 450°F/230°C/gas 8 for 5 minutes or until the meringue has browned.

Pears in Parcels

For the dough:
4oz/100g flour
4oz/100g butter
3oz/75g cheese, grated

salt
a little water

Rub the butter into the flour and stir in the grated cheese. Add a pinch of salt and enough water to make a light dough. Knead until smooth, and chill.

For the filling:

1 tin (1 lb/500 g) pears (or fresh pears, halved)	*butter, sugar and ground almonds mixed*

Roll out the dough thinly and cut into large squares. Put a drained pear into the middle of each square and put a mixture of butter, sugar and ground almonds into the cavity of each pear. Fold the pastry over and seal the moistened edges with a fork to make a parcel. Bake at 400°F/200°C/gas 6 for 20–25 minutes. Serve hot.

Chocolate Marshmallow Pie

⅜ *pint/200 ml milk*	*2 egg-whites, stiffly beaten*
4 oz/100 g marshmallows	*chocolate biscuit crust (see page 137)*
¼ *pint/150 ml double cream, whipped*	*grated chocolate*

Line an 8 in/20 cm flan dish with chocolate biscuit crust. Warm the milk and add the marshmallows. Stir until they melt. Remove from the heat and leave until half-set, beating from time to time (about ½ hour). Then fold in the whipped cream and the stiffly beaten egg-whites. Turn into the flan case and leave to set in the refrigerator. Decorate with grated chocolate.

Georgy Porgy Pudding

½ *Swiss roll*	½ *pint/300 ml milk*
2 eggs, separated	*grated lemon rind*
4 oz/100 g caster sugar	

Slice the Swiss roll and put into a well-greased flan dish. Beat the egg yolks with 2 oz/50 g of the sugar, then add the

milk and the lemon rind. Pour over the sliced roll, and bake
at 350°F/180°C/gas 4 for 15–20 minutes until set. Cool a little.
Beat the whites stiffly and add the rest of the sugar, beating
until very stiff. Pile on top of the pudding and return to the
oven for about 10 minutes to brown.

Jolly Jelly

6 satsumas   *1½ pint/1 l fresh orange juice*
1 packet gelatine   *cream*

Peel the satsumas and divide them into segments. Melt the
gelatine in a little of the orange juice over a low heat until it
has dissolved, then add to the rest of the juice. Arrange the
fruit decoratively in a glass dish and pour the juice gently
over it. Leave in a cool place to set and then either decorate
with cream or serve with Easy Ice Cream (see page 95).

Cheerful Cherry Bomb

Make some meringues (see page 79) and break them into
small pieces. Place them over the bottom of a dish. Cover
with scoops of vanilla ice cream and cover with a layer of
whipped cream. Put halved glacé cherries over the top and
serve chilled.

As a variation, pour a tin of black cherries, heated in their syrup, over the top just before serving.

Ice Cream Cake

Put thin slices of Swiss roll or any sponge cake in a dish and make 3 layers with vanilla ice cream. Cover with whipped cream, decorate with chopped glacé cherries and nuts, and serve immediately.

Some Basic Recipes: Sauces, Butters, Batter and Pastry

Sauces

Béchamel Sauce

1½ oz/40 g butter
2 tbs flour

½ pint/300 ml heated milk
salt and pepper

Melt the butter in a heavy saucepan. Gradually stir in the flour with a wooden spoon or whisk, then add the milk slowly, stirring all the time until the sauce thickens. Season to taste. Simmer very gently over a low heat for 10 minutes to allow the flour to cook. For a richer sauce add cream at the end of cooking.

Brown sauce

Add stock instead of milk to the béchamel (see above).

Sauce à la Crème

Add cream instead of milk to the béchamel (see above).

Mushroom Sauce

Add 4 oz/100 g sliced mushrooms, cooked lightly in butter, to the béchamel (see above). Simmer for 10 minutes until the sauce is mushroom-coloured.

Mild Mustard Sauce

Add approximately 1 tbs French mustard to the béchamel (see left) at the end of the cooking time, and allow to simmer for a few minutes to allow the flavour to permeate the sauce. The quantity of mustard used will depend on personal taste as well as the strength of the mustard.

Tomato Sauce

1 large onion, chopped
2 carrots, peeled and chopped
2 oz /50 g butter
1 large tin (1 lb /500 g) tomatoes (or
fresh), chopped

mixed herbs
½ pint /300 ml stock
salt and pepper

Sauté the onion and carrots in butter until they are very soft, about 10 minutes. Peel the tomatoes, if fresh and add, with their juices and the herbs to the pan and cook for a further 5 minutes. Add the stock and simmer until tender, about 10 minutes. Season to taste and liquidise.

Very Quick Tomato Sauce

Liquidise a medium tin (8 oz /225 g) of tomatoes with 1 small, finely chopped onion, herbs, salt and pepper. Heat through.

Onion Sauce

¾ pint /450 ml béchamel sauce
see above)

½ lb /250 g onions
melted butter

Peel the onions and boil them until soft. Chop them finely and toss in a little melted butter. Stir into the béchamel and simmer for 5–10 minutes.

Vinaigrette

1 tbs vinegar   garlic (optional)
1 tsp mustard   ¼ pint/150 ml olive oil
salt and pepper

Mix the vinegar and mustard in a small bowl and season with salt and pepper. Add crushed garlic to taste, if you want to include it as a flavouring. Add the olive oil gradually in a thin stream, stirring all the time until the vinaigrette thickens and amalgamates. Leave to stand for a while before dressing the salad so that the flavours permeate the oil.

Mayonnaise

2 egg yolks   ½ pint/300 ml vegetable
1 tsp dry mustard   oil
salt and pepper

Put the egg yolks into the blender and add the mustard, salt and pepper. Liquidise slowly, and then through the hole in

the top of the lid pour a thin stream of oil into the eggs. Stop pouring from time to time to let the mixture thicken. When the oil is all used up and the mayonnaise is thick, pour into a screw-top jar and keep in the refrigerator. Be sure to keep it no more than 1 week.

Butters

Garlic Butter

2 oz/50 g salted butter
1 large clove of garlic, peeled

Melt the butter in a pan and add the crushed clove of garlic. Stir for a few moments and then leave to settle for a while, or refrigerate until set.

Beurre Noisette

Melt some butter in a pan over a gentle heat and carry on cooking it until it foams and turns a lovely nut-brown colour. Serve at once. For such a simple sauce it has an incredible flavour and is worth trying with other recipes too, for example the Chicken Kebabs on page 121.

Pancake Batter

For 18–20 pancakes:

¾ pint/450 ml milk and water mixed	½ tsp salt
	8 oz/250 g sifted flour
4 eggs	2 oz/50 g butter, melted

Liquidise the water, milk, eggs and salt. Then add the flour and the butter. Blend for 1 minute. Thin out with milk if necessary. Cover and chill for 2 hours before using. To make dessert pancakes add sugar and use a thin batter. The pancakes can be made in batches and frozen between pieces of foil.

Here are some variations on a flan-case theme:

Savoury Flans

To bake blind: Line the pastry case with a piece of foil and fill with dried beans. Bake at 350°F/180°C/gas 4 for 20 minutes. Remove the foil and return the pastry to the oven for a few minutes to crisp up.

Oil Pastry

For an 8 in/20 cm flan case:
6 oz/175 g plain flour   *⅛ pint/75 ml vegetable oil*
½ tsp salt   *1½ tbs water*

Sieve the flour, add the salt, and stir in the oil and the water. Mix well and knead briefly until smooth. Do not chill or roll out. Press around the greased flan dish with your knuckles and bake blind.

Short Crust Pastry

For an 8 in/20 cm flan case:
4 oz/100 g flour   *2 oz/50 g butter or lard*
a large pinch of salt   *3–4 tbs cold water*

Sift the flour with the salt and rub in the fat lightly until it resembles breadcrumbs. Mix in the water and knead to a smooth dough on a cool surface. Cover and chill before using.

Savoury Crumb Crust

For an 8 in/20 cm flan case: *1½ oz/40 g butter*
4 oz/100 g cheese biscuit crumbs   *salt*

Melt the butter and add to the crumbs with the salt. Press into a greased flan dish and chill. Best with a cold filling, but it can be cooked.

Sweet Flans

Sweet Pastry Crust

For an 8in/20cm flan case:
3 oz/75 g butter	*3 tsp sugar*
6 oz/175 g flour	*up to 4 tbs cold water*

Rub the butter into the flour until it is crumb-like, then add the sugar and mix well. Add the water and knead the pastry on a floured surface until it is light and smooth. Chill for 2 hours before rolling out.

Biscuit Crust

For a 10in/25cm flan case:
8 oz/250 g Digestive or other biscuits	*4 oz/100 g butter*
	2–3 tbs sugar

Crush the biscuits to fine crumbs and melt the butter. Add the sugar to the crumbs and then mix with the melted butter. Press into greased flan dish and chill.

For variety you can add chopped nuts or grated chocolate to the crumbs before mixing with the butter.

Chocolate Biscuit Crust

For an 8–10in/20–25cm flan case:
12 Digestive biscuits	*2 tbs brown sugar*
3 oz/75 g butter	*2 oz/50 g plain chocolate, grated*

Crush the biscuits to fine crumbs. Melt the butter, sugar and grated chocolate and mix well. Line a greased flan dish and chill.

INDEX